Do any of the following mistakes sound familiar to you?
• Misinterpreting the attentions of the opposite sex.
• Finding it difficult to express your feelings to the
  woman you love.
• Thinking and talking too much about men.
• Feeling envious or jealous of your married friends.

If so, then don't think you're the only one who ever
commits these errors. Because these are among the *common*
mistakes that Christian singles make.

Mary Whelchel, a single woman and mother, is aware of
the pitfalls that ensnare divorced and never-married Christians. (She's fallen into a few herself.) In this honest,
insightful book, she identifies common errors and offers
practical solutions. Mary also confronts the mistakes others make in their attitudes toward singles.

Common Mistakes Singles Make is affirming and hopeful
yet direct in its approach to the problems most singles
share. You'll be reminded that God is always willing to
forgive you for your mistakes. With His loving encouragement and guidance, you can enjoy contentment as a
Christian single.

Common Mistakes Singles Make

MARY WHELCHEL

Fleming H. Revell
A Division of Baker Book House
Grand Rapids, Michigan 49516

Library of Congress Cataloging-in-Publication Data

Whelchel, Mary.
   Common mistakes singles make / Mary Whelchel.
      p.   cm.
   ISBN 0-8007-5296-1
   1. Single people—Religious life. 2. Single people—Conduct of life. 3. Whelchel, Mary.   I. Title.
   BV4596.S5W47   1989
   248.8′4—dc20   89-33866
                                                      CIP

To my daughter, Julie,
who has always made me look good as a mother.
You are a treasured gift from God to me—
undeserved, but much appreciated.

Contents

Preface

My natural tendency was *not* to write another book for singles, since as a single person myself, I'm a little tired of being constantly reminded in the Christian community that I'm single! I just want to be treated like a regular person, no better, no worse, no different.

But in the last few years as I've interacted with many singles through my radio ministry and speaking across the country, I have been made well aware that the majority of Christian single people are still struggling with some aspects of that singleness. (Just as marrieds are struggling with marriage!) As I've read their letters and talked with many single Christians, I've been amazed to see how many of us are in the same spot, worrying about the same things, making the same mistakes.

Not long ago I presented a radio program on "Common Mistakes of Single Women." I scheduled this program in the summer months, when listenership is usually down, thinking that its appeal would be minimal. I could not have been more mistaken. Our mailbox was flooded; we were inundated with letters and requests for the tape of that message.

The bells started to go off in my head, and I realized that though my message was very simple and plainspoken—or perhaps because of that—it had touched a chord in many people and seemed to give them hope and encouragement. I think the reason for the large response to that message is that many could say, "That's the way I feel. It's so good to know somebody else has done the same thing. I'm not all that weird!" One listener wrote: "Prior to hearing the message, I thought that I was the only single who went through these things."

We all recognize how helpful it is to know that others struggle where we struggle, others hurt as we do, others do the same dumb things we've done. But as Christians we need more than comrades in misery, more than fellow sufferers. We need victory; we need answers; we need relief. If Christians don't have solutions for the problems and difficulties of singleness, how can we recommend Christianity to others? If Christ is not sufficient to meet our needs as singles, how can we share with others that He can meet *their* needs?

For Christian singles to make the same mistakes over and over again and never find their way out of the labyrinth gives testimony to our world that Christ is not all we need, the Bible doesn't have every answer, and we can't handle these things any better than anybody else. That's not the Christian message, but that's the message of many Christian lives.

So, this book comes as a result of that radio program, and has been broadened to include all Christian singles, not just women. (I wouldn't want anyone to think that women make all the mistakes and men none!) I hope that as you read this book you will find yourself in some of its pages, and in so doing, you will find some road signs to lead you out of your particular labyrinth.

I write from experience. I've been a single mom for over fifteen years, out in the business world earning a living, trying to cope with my singleness, and making a great many of the mistakes you will read about here. Frankly, I could crawl under a chair when I think about some of the stupid things I've done. If it weren't for God's grace and forgiveness, I'm quite certain I never would have gotten over the guilt and remorse of the self-centered life I led for almost ten years.

But, praise His name, He's still in the business of turning ashes into beauty, and over the past six years, He's done an incredible job of that for me. So, if you feel as though you've blown it too often and too badly, remember me and be encouraged. If I'm salvable, anybody is.

This book is written for any Christian single, however you have been ushered into that category. In some cases it touches on areas that are common to almost all of us, and in others it speaks to more specific areas for never-marrieds or divorced, or certain age groups.

Wherever you fit, I encourage you to keep reading. Even if you don't agree with everything I say—and you surely won't—I believe you'll be encouraged. I hope you'll also be challenged in those areas where you've made too many mistakes too often.

I write as one single to another, as though we were having a cup of coffee together and chatting about our experiences. But most important, I write to give glory to my Lord and Savior, Jesus Christ, because He continues to deliver me from the many mistakes I make and to use me for His eternal purposes. If you haven't yet discovered the joy and contentment that come from finding your meaning in Jesus Christ, I pray this book will move you in that direction.

I think it might also be helpful to address the title of this book—*Common Mistakes Singles Make—How to recognize and prevent the problems that Christian singles encounter.* Why would I choose a title like that? Let me try to answer some of the questions the title may have brought up.

1. Do all singles make most of these mistakes?

I've never taken a statistically valid survey of Christian singles so I cannot give you research findings. My own experience and contact with many other singles tell me these are fairly common to all of us. But anytime you make generalizations, you will always have exceptions.

I conducted several focus groups of singles before writing this book, and by far the large majority of those singles related to most of these mistakes, if not for themselves personally, at least in their experience with other singles.

Some of these mistakes are preclusive; that is, if you make one, it would eliminate others. Some are more common at one stage of our lives than at others. Some relate to certain single types more than others.

It goes without saying that, like everyone else, we

singles come in all types and sizes. One size does not fit all. So I'll fall back on the old cliché, "If the shoe fits, wear it." And if it doesn't, just leave it for those who can relate to it.

2. Do Christian singles make more mistakes than non-Christian singles?

I seriously doubt it. I would hope, because we have the Holy Spirit of Christ dwelling within us, that we handle our circumstances much better and we have the power to resist and overcome which non-Christians lack.

So, why did I write a book about common mistakes of *Christians?* Because I'm a Christian; because Christians have different sources for answers than non-Christians. Since I've approached my single life from both perspectives—that is, from a non-Christian, secular approach and from a biblical approach—I think I understand the differences. I'm certain I understand which approach works and which one doesn't!

3. Do Christian singles make unique mistakes?

Yes and no. Many of our mistakes are the same ones we see in our single friends who don't know Christ. Some are unique, because they relate to our Christian community, our Christian principles, and our Christian culture.

4. Are these mistakes necessarily made only by singles?

Most of these mistakes are specifically related to the single life. But, with slight changes, they are in many cases the same mistakes married people make.

People are people. Having a marriage license and a mate doesn't change our basic personalities, nor does it automatically solve any problems. I'm quite certain that if married people read this book, they'll identify with many of the points and issues here.

Please let me make it clear that I don't think singles make more mistakes than anyone else. I certainly don't want to categorize us any more than has already been done. But our life-styles have some particular characteristics that are unique, and there's no denying that.

So, with all those explanations, disclaimers, and a bit of justification, I'll move ahead into those common mistakes of Christian singles.

Introduction

Throughout this book I draw heavily upon my own experiences as a single Christian. I think, therefore, it would be helpful to introduce myself to you a bit, so that you will know where I'm coming from, and the references throughout the book will make sense.

I have been "single again" for over fifteen years, having come into that category through divorce. My daughter was eight years old at the time, so I have worn those "single" or "single mother" labels for a long time. I'm sure no one plans on divorce as a part of his or her life pattern, but for me it was certainly a far cry from my own thinking and the kind of teaching and upbringing I had.

So, when I found myself a young single mother, I was not prepared for the world that awaited me. I had just completed a bachelor's degree in, of all things, piano performance, never intending to be a career woman, but rather to have an avocation of teaching piano, directing choirs, and other fun things! But here I was, faced with the necessity of earning enough money to keep Julie and me going, with a degree that offered little earning potential, and living in one of the most expensive areas of the country—Westchester County, New York.

Having spent a few years as a secretary with IBM, I went back there to find a job. I knew they were beginning to hire women in sales positions, and for some unexplainable reason, I thought I could sell. With a little persuasion and some good breaks, I was eventually able to convince IBM to give me a try. So, fresh out of a separation, with a music degree and no real business experience, knowing absolutely nothing about selling, I plunged into a world of men, in a job previously held only by men, truly unaware of what I was doing. Sometimes, though, stupidity pays off, because had I realized what lay ahead, I probably would have been too frightened to try!

Had I candidly expressed at that time what my plans were, I would have said they were to pursue this career and do the best job I could while waiting for the day when the right man would come along and rescue me. I was fairly certain that another marriage was in my future, somewhere, somehow. And that was what I wanted more than anything else—a man, to prove I was okay, to show the world Mary Whelchel wasn't a failure, to convince myself I could have a great marriage.

I was a Christian, having been raised in a wonderful Christian home down south and accepting Christ as my Savior in my early years. I had good Bible teaching all my life both from my churches and my parents. I attended and eventually graduated from a Christian college. My relationship with the Lord was sincere and founded on biblical truth, though much of that teaching and truth never came through into practice until very recently.

I was always active in my church, directing the choir, attending services every Sunday, and so on, and I never, thank God, severed those relationships. That early training held me to the church, even though my relationship with God started slipping quickly.

Feeling a desperate need to find a man, and also a great deal of guilt over being divorced, I began to think incorrectly. I thought that because God hates divorce, He would never allow me to be married again. To my thinking, that meant I would never know happiness. So, if I was to be married again, it would have to be against God's wishes, so to speak. And the desperate need I felt for marriage led me, rather subconsciously, to do it my way, as we say these days.

I simply started running my own show, doing whatever felt good, trying to find that relationship wherever I could (and certainly there were no eligible single men my age in my suburban church setting). I was surrounded by men in my business environment and getting a good bit of attention because I was one of the first females in that job. So the setting was ideal for me to become enamored with the world, with men in that world, and to seek self-fulfillment just as everyone else in my career-oriented environment was doing.

In addition, I was having some good measure of success in my career, selling pretty well, and recognition started coming my way, then a promotion, which led to some world travel. A second promotion required a move to Princeton, New Jersey; so I uprooted my dear daughter in her ninth grade, and off we went.

She adjusted beautifully, but Mom was becoming more

and more desperate. Five or six years had passed, and there were no wedding bells ringing. What was wrong with me? Where was Prince Charming?

I used to ask my friends, "Tell me the truth, what's wrong with me? Just tell me; I can handle it." And they would look at me with blank stares and shake their heads. "Nothing's wrong with you," they would say, but I wasn't convinced.

Oh, there were men in my life during those years. Nice men with impressive credentials, but certainly not God's choice for me. (I simply wasn't consulting God on anything at that point.) Trying to attract them and to be part of the scene, I let my "life-style slippage" become more and more drastic. My standards were lowered little by little; the principles of God were ignored inch by inch. As the years ticked by, anyone not knowing my background probably never would have known that I was a Christian. Very little in my life reflected Jesus Christ.

A couple of years after moving to Princeton I received a job offer from a good company in Chicago. Julie was entering her junior year; my career at IBM was on the verge of really breaking into some bigger territory; I knew no one in Chicago, had no friends or relatives there. Why would I even consider a move to Chicago at that stage in our lives?

Desperateness—that's why. In my heart of hearts, I thought, *Surely in Chicago, living in a big city like that, I will meet a man.* A relationship which I had thought was the right one had just fallen through, and I was coming to the end of my rope. So, against all good judgment for my daughter's well-being and my own career, I took the job and moved to Chicago. After all, at least it was a new scene.

We bought a lovely condo and the glamor of city living attracted both of us at first. We found a good school for Julie, and again by God's grace, she settled in well and quickly.

But Mom had some problems. The job wasn't what I thought it would be; in fact, it was a bit of a disaster. Look what I had given up, and I couldn't go back. What was I to do? I couldn't move Julie again.

Upon moving to Chicago I had started attending Moody Memorial Church, a church I had heard about all my life because of its great history. It was very convenient to our home, so it was the natural place to go. Thank God for that. My pastor's sermons began, little by little, to get through my thick skull.

Facing a career disaster, I was almost ready to turn back to God, but another relationship developed and side-tracked me for another year or so. Having found another good position, I thought I had things back under control again. My father has called me "Hardhead" all my life for good reason: I don't give up easily. I just kept thinking I could work my way out of anything that happened, and if I looked long enough, I'd find Mr. Wonderful.

When that relationship with a truly nice man didn't work out exactly as I wanted it to, my desperation returned, stronger than ever. I describe myself at that point as an emotional yo-yo, with dramatic highs and lows. And the emotional swings became more and more irrational and uncontrollable.

How well I remember the night I decided I could no

longer deal with this relationship, not because the gentle-
man I was seeing had done anything wrong. Indeed, he
had not, though there was no question that our relationship was not right, since we did not share a common belief
and faith in Jesus Christ. But I now know it was the Holy
Spirit working so intensely within me that caused me to
break off the relationship. So, in the middle of the night,
I went to my friend's house and told him it was over. I had
no reason that made any sense to him or to me. I kept
thinking, *Why are you doing this? This may be your last
chance.* But I was driven to it.

After an all-night conversation, I went home, picked up
my Bible, and started reading it for the first time in years—
ten years to be exact. That day began my pursuit of God.
A few days later I finally could pray, "Okay, Lord, I'll be
anything You want me to be; I'll even be single forever if
You'll just give me peace. I can't live without Your peace
any longer."

Those words came slowly and painfully for me. I was
frightened, for I knew God might take me at my word,
and I really didn't want to be single. Though I knew
immediate relief from the terrible struggle inside me, the
pain did not end overnight. Not by a long shot. Days and
weeks and months of painful relinquishment lay ahead of
me, and the battle to live out what I had committed to God
became a daily, moment-by-moment, sometimes excruci-
atingly difficult experience.

I turned to God's Word and prayer. I couldn't get
through the day without it. Many times I came close to
reneging on my commitment, as the pain of watching my
dreams die seemed overwhelming. But each time, the

Holy Spirit would whisper to me, "Can't you trust Me? I do have good plans for you. Please, trust Me."

The journals I began keeping at that time chronicle those days of giving up. The spiritual growth I experienced was incredible; the lessons I learned are invaluable to this day. Thank God for all that teaching I'd had all those years; it was lying there dormant, waiting for a little water to take life again. And it came back to me in rapid fashion.

As each day and week passed, the peace of God began more and more to rule in my life, and I knew I was hooked. This was living; I could never go back to that self-controlled, self-centered life again. Although the pain of giving up lasted for a while (eighteen months) the blessedness of knowing that I was in right relationship to Jesus Christ and the contentment He was imparting to me through His Word were beyond description.

That period led me to establish a strong daily time each morning with the Lord. I didn't do it because it was some legal requirement. I did it out of desperation—I needed the Word of God and His presence to make it through my days. And the time began expanding, as I wanted more and more. Thank God for that discipline, because it has made all the difference, and it continues to be true in my life. It is only God's Word that can work miracles in us, and it takes time to pour it in.

With that inpouring of God's Word and through prayer, my thinking started changing; my desires started changing. I would never have guessed my desire to be married could ever really change. I figured I would somehow just be able to live with this unfulfilled desire without going crazy, but it was asking too much to think my desires might actually be changed.

That was a little over six years ago. My, what six years has wrought! Had God cured me of cancer, the miracle could not be greater. He changed me when I thought it would be impossible to do so. And the past six years have been an exciting adventure, to see what He's going to do next with this one single, divorced woman, who made a shambles of her life and deserved nothing good whatsoever.

A ministry I had started for working women in my wonderful church led, through a miracle, to my starting a weekly radio program, "The Christian Working Woman," on a station in Chicago. After six months, it was not just 1 station, but 6, and eventually a daily program was added to the weekly program. As I write this, we are heard on over 135 stations across the country.

Soon after I began the ministry, God made it possible for me to become self-employed. I am still a Christian working woman, earning my own living through business training seminars in the fields of customer service skills, telemarketing, telephone skills, guest relations training, sales training, and so on. Basically, my biggest challenge is the balancing act between working enough to pay my bills and having time left to manage the ministry, write, and still be a mother, mother-in-law, daughter, sister, aunt, and friend!

I am now a truly contented single person. But that doesn't mean I don't have moments when I long for the companionship of a man. Of course I do, and sometimes those desires are strong. But through these past six years,

I've learned some important lessons about walking with God, and thankfully I'm beginning to learn to have "forever eyes," which cause me to see this earthly life in very different ways than before. It's a very short time we spend here, and the only things that count are those that last for eternity.

Will I ever marry again? I don't really know, though my guess would be probably not. I know there are different interpretations of Scripture concerning remarriage, so that would require careful consideration. However, at this point it is a moot question, and I don't waste time worrying about it. I don't pray for it at all, since I don't see it as a need anymore. But if in God's wisdom marriage would enable me and my husband to serve God more effectively than we can as single people, that's fine with me. I'm not fighting it, but I very much appreciate my single life-style and enjoy the freedom it offers me to pursue the opportunities that have come my way.

I readily recognize that my single status is different from that of others; we are all unique, no two of us are alike. It's true I have known what it is to be married, and I do have my wonderful daughter, which certainly satisfies some of those common longings singles feel. My personal experience will not relate to each of yours, but through these fifteen years of singleness, I've observed a great deal.

Through the ministry I have many opportunities to get to know single people, and that gives me a breadth of understanding I wouldn't have otherwise. I've been associated closely with singles ministries in churches, and, at one point, I headed our singles program at my large church, while the church was in the process of seeking a minister of singles. Those six or eight months gave me some intensive exposure to singles.

Though I hate to admit it, there are enough years under my belt now to give me some good perspective, I think. Though please be assured I haven't been around so long that I'm over the hill!

So, from that background, I have written this book, with one prayer: that God would use it in the lives of a few people to help them learn, easier and sooner than I did, that singleness is not a curse, and that God can salvage your life wherever it is. He is absolutely masterful at turning ashes into beauty and making gardens out of deserts. He continues to do that in my life.

Common
Mistakes
Singles
Make

1

Common Mistakes in Our Attitudes Toward Marriage

"I know, like you said, God wants me to seek him and his Word and take advantage of my time alone. But please pray for (1) the grace for me to do that, and (2) a Christian husband for me before I get much older. Being left single after serving God since I was eighteen really hurts. I see others who aren't even Christians blessed with husbands."

"I need to trust that God will provide for a lifetime partner. My Christian circle is limited, and from what I can see, I don't have many choices left. Anxiety is building around me from family and society. I deal with the anxiety in the best way I can, but still in my humanness, I feel alone and have a longing and desire to have a family, the way God intended."

"I thought life begins at forty, but I feel so depressed. All my friends are getting married and I seem to always be sitting on the sidelines watching others have their dreams come true."

*"I feel in my heart he's really the one. I know that if it's
ordained by God it will be forever. The problem is, I want to
be married NOW!"*

*"This time last year I was worried that I would never get
married again. I don't anymore. I still would like to, and I
think it's okay to say it, but I don't worry about it."*

* * *

This sample of excerpts from letters I have received from
singles is a collage of typical feelings and attitudes about
marriage.

No question about it, marriage is the highest priority for
many singles. The topic of marriage and having a family
seemed to be the predominant area of interest and struggle for my focus groups. So, I figured we'd start with this
one, and I hope it will be downhill from here!

**Mistake: We think marriage is the only normal life-style
and that it will solve all our problems.**

Single people frequently view their single status as one big
waiting room, waiting for "Mr. or Ms. Right" to come
along and rescue them from a fate more horrible than
death—being single!

There is a very common tendency to think that life
hasn't really begun for us yet. We're just marking time,

flying around in a holding pattern, waiting for this pre-requisite—marriage—before life can truly start. Even though many singles protest that they aren't doing this, they are.

There are reasons for this common attitude. Our society is built for twos. Although the majority of adults are now single, everything around us is designed for couples.

Try taking a vacation one to a room. Everything is priced and promoted as "double occupancy." Go into a really nice restaurant and eat by yourself. There are no tables for one, heads turn to watch you follow the maitre d' (usually to the back of the room), as though a single diner is a rare creature, and the waiter probably hates having you at his table because the tip will be smaller!

I live alone in a section of town houses designed for couples and families. There are only two or three of us singles living in the whole subdivision. How often people say to me, "Do you live here by yourself?" taking the inflection up at the end of the sentence as if to say, "Why in the world would anyone want to live here alone? This is designed for couples and families."

These are just a few examples of how our society is oriented to couples, not singles, and those subtle messages get through to us, as we encounter them day in and day out. It's not necessary for someone to say outright, "You don't fit into this society; you're single." Very few people would say that or admit to feeling that way. But the messages are all around us, and we single people are pretty smart; we don't miss them.

Now, there's no question that this is beginning to

change, as society is forced to cope with all us singles. But changes in attitudes come slowly. Ideas have been bred in, and you don't get rid of them quickly.

In addition, as Christian singles we face this attitude in our Christian community. Evangelical Christianity has a strong belief in the family (and well it should), which tends to produce an unfortunate and unnecessary countermessage: "You have to be married to be okay." This feeling is very obvious in the attitude taken toward singles in many churches. Seldom are they considered as board members, elders, deacons. But as soon as an active single person in a church gets married, he or she is asked to do many jobs that were not offered previously. Again, this is changing, but these changes, as we said before, come very slowly.

How many of us have to cope with family members who are saying to us, "You're not married yet?" I remember a remark made by a family member to my daughter before she was married, still unattached, which was something like, "But you're so pretty. What's wrong with those guys in Chicago?" The implication being that if you're pretty, you certainly should be married.

Sometimes the messages are subtle; sometimes they're right up front. But either way, it's true that families have bred these attitudes into us from our youngest years. "Grow up; get married. If you don't, something's wrong."

The balanced biblical view on this is rarely found. I hope I will be able to appropriately describe that balance. I'll begin by emphatically stating that I believe in marriage; it is a God-given institution. It is blessed and ordained by God for many good reasons. In Genesis 2:18 we read that

God gave us each other to create the companionship we need and eliminate loneliness. Obviously another key reason is to propagate the race by bearing children. Marriage produces families, which are the most intimate of support groups. We need those family relationships desperately. We can see all around us today the results of the breakdown in families.

So, as a Christian community, we should do everything we can to support families and build healthy marriages. That is a most important function of the Body of Christ.

But in doing that, there really is no reason we must create a backlash attitude which tells single people that singleness is a subnormal life-style. In some of the letters I paraphrased at the beginning of this chapter you can hear that attitude coming through: "God intended for everyone to be married and have a family. When that doesn't happen, life is dreary, God is unfair, and I've been shortchanged."

First Corinthians 7 is rarely used for sermon material. It doesn't fit in too well with this common idea that God intended marriage for everyone and anything else is second best. I will simply quote a few verses from that chapter:

> I would like you to be free from concern. An unmarried man is concerned about the Lord's affairs—how he can please the Lord. But a married man is concerned about the affairs of this world—how he can please his wife—and his interests are divided. An unmarried woman or virgin is concerned about the Lord's affairs: Her aim is to be devoted to the Lord in both body and spirit. But a

married woman is concerned about the affairs of this world—how she can please her husband. I am saying this for your own good, not to restrict you, but that you may live in a right way in undivided devotion to the Lord. . . . So then, he who marries the virgin does right, but he who does not marry her does even better.

1 Corinthians 7:32–35, 38

Often people say to me, "I don't understand how you do all the things you do. Where do you find the time?" I am able to do all the things I do to a great extent because I'm single. I don't have to worry about having a meal on the table each evening, so I use that time for other activities. I can get up at four in the morning and start writing without disturbing anyone. I can stay up until 2:00 A.M. to clean the house without upsetting anybody's schedule. I can spend hours alone reading and meditating on Scripture, shutting out all other distractions, without hurting anyone's feelings. I do not have to be concerned about those things, and there's no guilt to carry around because I've neglected a relationship.

One night recently, my parents were visiting and I just had to work late on ministry business. The ministry's office is one of the bedrooms in my home, located next to the guest room. The printer was running until 2:00 A.M., and I was very worried about disturbing their sleep. In the midst of all that, I realized that I do this kind of thing all the time, but I never have to worry about disturbing anyone else. There's a freedom in my singleness which, when used correctly, gives me more time for ministry than I would have otherwise.

Now, I also recognize that I miss out on the many joys and pleasures shared by two people who are married. There is loneliness to cope with at times, and that feeling which sometimes creeps in to remind me I'm not the most important person in the world to some one person. There are vacations I'd like to take and restaurants I'd like to eat in which I've postponed because I don't have just the right person to do it with.

Yes, there are pluses and minuses, assets and liabilities. But what we singles forget is that this is true of the other side of the fence, too. There are negative aspects to marriage, even a good marriage. I can assure you that many happily married people look at my freedom with some envy at times. They simply realize that they have the joys of marriage, which I lack, but they also have the responsibilities, which I don't have.

The key thing we need to understand is that God has not advocated one life-style—marriage—as the number one, normal way to live, and the other life-style—single-ness—as second-best leftovers for those who missed the marriage boat for some reason or another.

Let me remind you of some people in Scripture who were either certainly or most likely single: Jesus, the Apostle Paul, Lazarus and his sisters, Mary and Martha, Lydia, Mary Magdalene, Dorcas. Many others are never referred to as married and have life-styles that would lead you to think they were probably single, including some of the disciples and many in the early church.

I know you probably know all this, but somewhere in the thought process, we still forget to put these facts into the equation when we think about getting married. We keep an attitude that says, "You have to be married to live a normal life!"

There are some dangers in allowing ourselves to think that marriage is the only normal life-style and it will solve all our problems. First of all, you place an unduly heavy responsibility and expectation on marriage, which it will not be able to live up to. You're setting yourself up for disappointment and failure, if and when you do get married.

Second, you're asking too much of that other person who will be your mate. Even if you marry the most wonderful person in the world, he or she will not be able to meet your needs totally. To expect so much is to invite disaster.

Third, a person consumed with the desire to be married usually becomes less and less attractive because that message is unconsciously transmitted through body language, facial expressions, conversation, and the like. It's a perfume that exudes from every pore, and you can smell it a mile off! This often produces a Catch-22 situation: The stronger the desire, the less attractive one becomes, which creates a desperateness and an even stronger desire.

Finally, when we think of marriage as an essential, we start to make an idol out of it. It becomes more important to us than anything else. That's idolatry, and God simply does not tolerate idolatry in our lives. He is a jealous God, and He demands first place in our thoughts, our ambitions, our desires, our devotion. When anything or anyone else starts to usurp that primary allegiance, we are into idolatry. We can expect trouble.

Any desire, even a legitimate one, can become an idol. You won't have to look far to see Christians who have allowed legitimate, worthwhile desires to control them and disrupt the lordship of Jesus Christ in their lives. I see people making idols of family, of church work, of ministries. And, oh, I see so many singles who've allowed this normal desire to be married to become the central focus of their lives. And when that desire is out of control, several other telltale symptoms usually accompany it:

• Emotional highs and lows, depending upon whether or not there's a prospect on the scene.
• Decreased spiritual emphasis. Not much time in God's Word or prayer. Not much desire to talk about spiritual things.
• Minimal outreach to others. Little involvement in other people's problems. Lack of awareness of others' problems or hurting.
• Exaggerated concern about looks and appearance.

Well, what do we do? Throw up our hands and quit? Leave the human race? Put our heads in the sand and ignore? Join the nearest monastery? Pray for the gift of celibacy?

None of the above. We go back to Matthew 6:33 and practice it: "But seek first his kingdom and his righteousness, and all these things will be given to you as well." Does that verse say we'll get our marriage partner if we seek first God's Kingdom? No, it says we'll get what we need, and God knows what we need better than we do.

You know this verse; you've probably got it memorized by now. You've heard dozens of sermons on it. But do you practice it?

Seeking God first means that He is number one in your thinking, in your planning, in your priorities, in your desires. If you seek first the Kingdom of God, I promise you that you will not be consumed with a desire to be married—or any other desire, for that matter. You will not make the mistake of thinking that marriage is the answer to all your problems. You will not exhibit the symptoms listed a few paragraphs back.

If you're a single person who struggles with this mistaken attitude toward marriage, you're the only one who can change that. Society won't help you; the church can't do it for you; your family may never change their view. But you *can* change, if you recognize the error in your thinking and start programming your mind to think biblically.

I did not say you would *lose* your desire to be married, but rather that you would no longer be consumed by it. You'll know there is purpose and meaning in what you're doing as a single person. The thought of never being married won't send you into a panic attack.

Let me hasten to add that you can still have moments when that desire seems overwhelming and out of control. But at those moments, the critical test is where do you turn? Do you hightail it back to the Word of God pretty quickly, praying and seeking God's power over that desire? Or do you start to bog down in the mire again?

Many Christian singles go in and out of victory on this issue regularly, and you can usually tell which way the wind's blowing. My guess is those periods are directly related to time spent in God's presence:

> Regular, consistent time with God = Desires under control of God's Spirit.
>
> Lack of consistent communion and fellowship with God = Desires consume us.

That may appear too simplistic for the tastes of some, but I am totally convinced it is true. God's Word bears out that message.

I am additionally convinced because I've experienced both. I am not simply an observer of singles making this mistake; I spent ten years determined to find the right man to marry, convinced that was the answer to my life's problems. I should have known better; I had good biblical teaching throughout my life. But in my determined manner, I insisted on doing it my way.

Let me tell you where my way got me. I was self-focused and self-centered; my spiritual life deteriorated quickly. My life-style was increasingly worldly, displeasing to the Lord, and damaging to my testimony. I felt frustrated and desperate most of the time. There were extreme emotional highs and lows, eventually leading to more and more lows and very few highs. I neglected relationships, as my own supposed needs for male companionship took precedence over everything else. Most important, I lost ten years of effective service for the Lord which can never be recaptured.

I don't live in regret, though, because my Savior has promised to restore "the years that the locust hath eaten"

(Joel 2:25 KJV) and He has turned my ashes into beauty (Isaiah 61:3), nonetheless I would surely do it differently if I could. And I would be ever so thankful if I could persuade a few of you reading this book to avoid this typical and all-too-common mistake made by Christian singles.

I struggle with ways to say this that won't sound trite or cliché-ridden. But here's the message: Only Jesus Christ is capable of meeting our needs, and that is no accident. God intended it to be that way. You are designed in such a way that you cannot be completely satisfied with anyone or anything except Jesus Christ. It's easy to understand why: He is the perfection of all of God's glory, and there is no possible way He can ever disappoint us. He's promised never to leave us or forsake us, and no one else can give us that promise. He says He'll be everything we need, and He has the power to make good on His promise. No one else can.

Sometimes I even feel that my singleness gives me an opportunity to know Christ in ways I might never have otherwise. Because I don't have someone here all the time to talk to, I can turn that into an opportunity to talk with the Lord more often, to learn to turn to my Wonderful Counselor more readily. Because there's not a mate in my life to occupy some of my time and devotion, my relationship with Jesus can occupy more of my time and devotion than it would otherwise. And in that process I discover that my deepest needs are met.

I can hear some of you thinking, *Yeah, I've heard all that stuff, but Jesus isn't here in the flesh. I can't touch Him or talk to Him face-to-face. It's just not the same.*

This reminds me of the story of the little boy who was afraid of the dark. As his father was putting him to bed one evening, he said, "Son, there's no reason for you to be afraid of the dark. Jesus is right here with you." The boy answered, "Yeah, I know, Dad, but I want someone with skin on!"

You want someone with skin on, too. I know. I have those same feelings at times. I want to feel an arm around me; I want to hear a voice saying, "I love you"; I want to snuggle in front of a cozy fire on a cold night with a real person. I'm glad I still have those feelings and desires because they're quite normal. We read in Genesis 2:18 that God said, "It is not good for the man to be alone. I will make a helper suitable for him." Part of our natural makeup, designed by our Creator, is to desire companionship with the opposite sex.

So, the happy medium here is to recognize these normal desires, accept them, and understand them, but not allow them to control you. And be willing to allow God to direct your life in either direction—married or single. That's turning the controls over to God without a preplanned agenda.

Few people do that. Few singles ever give God permission to direct them to a life of singleness. They cannot imagine that life could be meaningful without marriage, and they simply refuse to give God the opportunity to show them anything else. I did just that for ten years.

I remember a young woman in her late twenties, never married, who attended a workshop I gave at a singles conference. I had tried to point out that we must relinquish to God our right to be married, and believe that if singleness is His plan for us, we won't be just okay, we'll be better than we could ever be any other way.

Afterwards this young woman said to me, "But I just can't believe I could ever be happy any way except married. I don't see how that would be possible. I want to be married so badly." I answered, "You don't have to understand how God will work this out in your life if indeed it is His will for you to be single. You simply have to be willing to let Him. Will you just unlock those clenched fists right now and say, 'God, though frankly I don't think it's possible for me to be happy or complete unless I'm married, I'm willing to turn it over to You. If You want me to be single then somehow You'll have to work a miracle that is beyond my imagination, and make me contented to be single. But I give You permission to do that if that is Your will.' "

It's not an easy prayer. But it is the ultimate prayer of submission every Christian must pray if Jesus is going to be Lord of our lives. It is this death to self and our own desires and plans that every Christian must realize if he ever truly becomes a disciple. For many singles, that point of submission is their desire to be married. When we refuse to give that up, we know that marriage has become an idol for us.

But please let's not forget the other side of this coin. Jesus said when we lose our lives, we find them. This submission to God, even to be single if that's what He wants, does not lead us into a life of dreariness and loneliness, martyrs for Jesus. No, that's when we discover what the word *life* really means.

The words I finally said six years ago were, "Lord, I'll do

anything You want, I'll even be single forever, if You'll just give me peace!" I fought ten long miserable years against that act of submission, and I was at the end of my emotional rope before I gave in. I don't give up easily, but thank God for His stubborn love which never gave up on me and kept me from the plans I was so determined to pursue.

There is simply no way to compare the last six years with those ten years of struggle. Oh, I went through some painful months as I watched my dream die. It didn't just wilt overnight, no pain, no problem. It took about eighteen months before I knew I was totally delivered from my consuming desire to be married. But even those eighteen months were wonderful, because my fellowship with the Lord was so sweet. There is *nothing* to compare with peace and contentment. Once you get a taste of the peace that Jesus gives when He has control of every area of your life, you shake your head and wonder how you ever could have been so dumb and stupid as to think you could run your own show and figure out the best plan for your life.

I gave up my desires and gave the controls to Jesus; I thought it would be the worst thing in the world but I saw no other options. I know now that by doing that, I have found life, the abundant life that we're supposed to have as Christians. To be rid of the guilt that plagued me for those ten years, to go to bed at night knowing God is pleased with my life-style, to discover that I'm changing on the inside in ways I thought I never could, to know that I'm being used by God to help others, to be involved in activities that have eternal significance—those are a few of the benefits I gained by giving up and dying! Not a bad exchange!

2

Common Mistakes in Relating to the Opposite Sex

"Recently I suffered through a very short engagement with a man I have known for eight years. . . . As you explained, there were so many warning signs, but I continued to ignore them, foolishly hoping that things would get better. . . . As my wedding date neared, I found myself compromising my stand as a Christian woman. . . . To make a long story short, I am no longer engaged but there is a tremendous amount of peace in my heart."

"God has given me a very nice young man who is very much in love with me and wants to marry me. We have been going together for only four weeks. . . . But the one thing that frightens me is that our relationship has a lot of sexual drive. I have always wanted to save myself for my wedding night, but the excuse he gives me is that he's going to marry me anyway. Why not now?"

"I was married for almost twenty years and have now been single for three and a half years. I have gone through a few relationships that were not God's choice. . . .

Slowly — very slowly — I am becoming content with my life as a single."

"In November I found out I was pregnant and became very distressed because I'm not married. Well, I want to report that everything went just fine with the delivery and a beautiful adoption arrangement with an exceptional Christian family. It's been four months now and the comfort of God is ever prevalent. . . . I would like to share a suggestion about hints on being single: No matter how much you feel it will please the man you're seeing, don't have sex before marriage."

* * *

These are some additional comments from singles who are struggling to relate to a man or woman. No question about it, the opposite sex occupies a great deal of our thought and time as a rule, whether we have a special person in our lives or not. With the God-given attraction that we have for the opposite sex, there seem to come many problems for singles which are surely not God-given!

Let's look at some of the more common ones.

Mistake: We misinterpret the attentions of the opposite sex.

As an outgrowth of the frustration and desperateness sometimes experienced when we want to be married, many singles overreact to any attention from someone of the opposite sex, especially if that someone is attractive to them. If a man looks at us twice, we women can read all kinds of things into it. If a woman happens to sit by a man at a social function, he thinks she's sending him come-ons. These advances have one of two effects: We like the person and respond positively, or we think he or she is being pushy and run the other way, depending upon whether we're attracted to that person or not.

I've seen extreme cases where singles have made fools of themselves by misinterpreting some attention and hanging on to a person like a leech. It can be very uncomfortable to try to extricate yourself from that predicament without being too obvious or embarrassing the "leech." On the other hand, there's the case where a single assumes a come-on that was nothing more than a friendly gesture (inflated ego?), and overreacts, to everyone's embarrassment.

You're probably misinterpreting attentions from others if you sit around with friends, discussing and justifying your misinterpretations, or even if you allow yourself to think these types of rationalizations:

> "Yes, but he talked with me for over fifteen minutes. He didn't have to talk with me that long. I'm sure he really likes me."

> "But you didn't see how she looked at me. A woman doesn't look at you like that if she's not sending a signal. I'm sure she wants to see me."

This misinterpretation of attentions is one of the major

reasons it's difficult for a single man and woman to have a platonic relationship. Both are on their guard, worried about signals, instead of allowing that two people can actually have a friendly conversation and enjoy each other's company without a romantic attraction.

I also observe too often that many singles—yes, Christian singles—enjoy sending signals and then disowning them. After all, it's an ego trip to think that one or two people are "on your string," hoping you'll come their way sooner or later, even if they're not attractive to you. So, in deceptive ways, they disguise their maneuvers (perhaps even to themselves) by telling everyone, "We're just friends." They even say that to the other person right up front, laying the groundwork for a quick exit when necessary, and then proceed to give attentions and signals that are truly misleading. Anyone would misinterpret them. And they break not a few hearts in the process of feeding their egos.

You are well advised to bend over backwards to avoid misinterpreting the attention of someone else. Make a slight change in the adage "When in doubt, don't," and tell yourself, "When in doubt, forget it." Assume, if there's any room for uncertainty, that you're pushing the limits and imagining things that are not there.

The key here is to stop thinking about it. Don't discuss your interpretations of his or her attentions with your friends; don't allow your mind to dwell on them. As soon as you do, they get blown out of proportion, and there you go. Control your reaction at the thought level; that's where it all starts. If you don't think about what those attentions might mean, you won't misinterpret them.

A word to the men: Control that tendency to think that every Christian woman is looking for a Christian man, so therefore, when she smiles at you, she's laying her trap. That is, after all, a rather proud line of thinking, and believe me, it's not always true! You need to change your reaction at the thought level, too.

Do yourself a favor and avoid some embarrassing moments by disciplining your thought life and not allowing yourself to misinterpret attentions from members of the opposite sex.

Mistake: We put up with too much in a relationship and hang on too long.

I once received a letter from a woman who had endured many years of really poor treatment from a man she was dating. It was obvious that he didn't want to give up the relationship, but neither did he want to pursue it. So, he kept her on a string for over ten years, playing with her like a puppet. He would lead her on to think he was getting serious about marriage, and then start dating someone else and flaunting it. She kept taking him back, not even voicing her displeasure with his behavior, afraid to do anything that would cause him to leave for good.

He would say things to her that were very cruel, intentionally hurting her. He learned that he could abuse the relationship any way he pleased, and she would put up with it. So, he did.

Even after all that, she wrote me to ask how to get him to marry her and stop these games he was playing. She thought she was truly in love with him and couldn't live without him. So she put up with too much and hung on too long.

Having done the same thing (though not to those extremes), I know what it feels like. Degrading—that's what it feels like. But you feel trapped because you can't stand the thought of not having a relationship. So you convince yourself that you really love him or her, and that's why you hang on.

I wish I had a nickel for every time someone has said to me something like, "I'd break up with him [or her] if I could, but I just can't do it. I know he's no good for me, but how can I live without him?"

The "fat lady has sung" in a great many of your relationships, but you're not willing to admit the opera is over. Do yourself a favor: Admit you have an emotional dependency you're calling "love"—or even admit that you really love the person if you think you do—but acknowledge that it's a wrong relationship and get out.

How do you get out? By taking drastic steps. Jesus said, "If your right eye causes you to sin, gouge it out and throw it away. It is better for you to lose one part of your body than for your whole body to be thrown into hell. And if your right hand causes you to sin, cut it off and throw it away. It is better for you to lose one part of your body than for your whole body to go into hell" (Matthew 5:29, 30). In the case of the woman who had taken abuse for over ten years, I advised her to change churches, because with such a long-term dependency, she really has to make certain she doesn't have to see him every time she goes to church.

I recently talked with a woman who has an emotional dependency on a man who mistreats her and the relationship; additionally, it has been a sinful relationship. I advised her to move far away—as far as is necessary to ensure she'll never see him again.

Drastic steps! Much better, however, than trying to end the relationship knowing the person is close by, seeing him frequently, and so on. I once decided to end an emotional dependency. I thought I couldn't do it, but I did. As soon as I took the step, the most incredible calm and peace came over me. Just knowing you've done the right thing brings immediate relief.

However, I didn't take drastic steps, and I allowed that person to work his way back into my life for a short while after that. Dumb, really dumb. When you're involved in a relationship that has had an emotional stronghold on you, you'll need some time to recover. You can't trust yourself. So, take drastic steps or you'll find your resolution to end it is very weak. With the slightest aggressiveness on the part of the other person, you'll give in. Or you may even become the aggressor.

If you're in a relationship and you're being treated with disrespect, thoughtlessness, or unkindness, that's a good sign you've hung on too long and put up with too much. If you're hoping he or she will change, you don't know too much about human nature. The one thing that might make a person like this change is having to live with the consequences of his or her behavior—namely, losing the relationship. As long as he or she can get by with treating you shabbily, there's not likely to be much change in behavior.

If you're not happy with the treatment you're receiving

from a person before you marry, you can be sure the treatment you would get after marriage would be much more of the same and worse.

When you know it's over, or you know it never should have started, have the respect for yourself and your testimony for Christ to get out of that relationship and stay out. If you're thinking you can't do it, you don't know the reality of Philippians 4:13: "I can do everything through him who gives me strength." Something's wrong with your relationship with Jesus Christ if you feel powerless to break another relationship that you know should be broken.

Mistake: We're not always very good at reading danger signals in a relationship.

I often see single people in relationships that have *poor choice* written all over them, but somehow they never seem to see the danger signals. The truth is, most of the time they just don't want to see them.

Remember that when our emotions get involved in a situation, it's very easy to lose perspective. Someone once told me, "Emotions and feelings have zero IQ," and I think that's a good thing to remember. You cannot trust your emotions. They're dumb sometimes! Those juices get flowing, those romantic notions start whirling around in your head, and you can lose perspective in an instant.

Not too long ago one of my dear nephews fell in love with a very nice young girl. And he fell hard. As he was telling me about her, I became concerned because she was very young. "Remember, all of us change a lot during these years," I said. "She will change, so you need to take your time." I prayed over the intervening months for the relationship. Not too long afterwards it did come to an end, and it was painful for him. But he wrote to say, "Aunt Mary, you were right. She changed a lot." Well, that was a danger sign—not just an age difference, but a young age where there was much more time needed for maturing.

As a happy ending to that story, he's now found the girl God was preparing for him, and they recently married. She's in his age category, mature, and they complement each other beautifully. No danger signals to worry about.

A few years ago a dear friend got engaged to a young man, and all of us who knew them saw many danger signals. "I know you're not really pleased about this, are you?" she asked. And I answered, "I'm not saying it won't work. I'm saying if it does, you will have bet against all the odds, so to speak, and won." But, my friends, she didn't win. She is now in a difficult marriage, isolated from all her friends and family.

Let's list a few of those danger signals:

Significant age difference. This will vary depending on individuals and depending on the ages involved. A forty-five-year-old person marrying someone ten years older or younger is much less risky than a twenty-five-year-old marrying someone that much older or younger, because so much change occurs during the late teens and twenties. By the late thirties those changes are not nearly as significant, as a rule. I'm not saying that age difference is always a problem, but it certainly is one thing you should consider carefully.

Different family upbringing. It's a fact that no two families are alike, so there are bound to be differences in any two families. But look at the basics: Were both families Christian? What values were taught by the families? What kind of relationships exist among the family members? Some families are very close and some are not. If you're used to a close family relationship, you may have difficulty being married to someone who sees no value in going to Grandma's for Christmas or giving birthday gifts or making phone calls to your cousin.

Different cultural interests. They tell us that Prince Charles and Lady Di are running into some difficulties in their storybook marriage. There is a fairly wide division in their ages, by the way, and in addition, he is oriented toward classical interests and she is oriented toward more faddish and contemporary interests. Not much in common, they say. Well, it can cause a problem.

Different attitudes toward children. Some people love them and want them around; others prefer to admire them from a distance and are not comfortable with children. It's very important to make sure you're compatible in this area.

Priority of spiritual life. If one person in the relationship puts a higher priority on spiritual life than the other, it's a real danger signal and should not be ignored. Usually when you are involved with someone whose spiritual temperature is below your own, you don't bring them up to your level, you go down to theirs. I've seen it time and again.

Mistake: We get physically involved much too soon and
*   go too far.*

Just a few days ago I had a letter from a single woman who
told me that she was depressed because the night before
she had gone to bed with a Christian man whose motives
she knew were strictly selfish. What I saw in her attitude
is alarming to me. The remorse was not over the sin so
much as over his motives. It seemed that if she had felt
this man really cared for her and there was a future in the
relationship, she would not have felt badly about the
sexual encounter.

Here again we Christians have allowed the world system and philosophy to infiltrate our thinking about the
physical aspects of a relationship. Romans 12:1, 2 says we
are not to be conformed to this world, but transformed by
a renewed mind. The Phillips translation says ". . . Don't
let the world around you squeeze you into its own
mould." When we become casual about having sex before
marriage, we've been shoved into the world's mold.

The Bible is explicit: Sex is for within the boundaries of
marriage, nothing else, no exceptions. I recognize that is
out-of-date thinking to this world system, but so what?
Anytime your thinking is in line with the majority, you'd
better stop and check it out because nine times out of ten
the majority's thinking is not biblical. A dear non-
Christian friend laughed at me when I explained my view
that sex is for within the boundaries of marriage. It was
just the most foolish philosophy he'd ever heard, and he
reminded me that I'm totally out of step with society, and
besides, it's impossible to be single and go without sex.

That's what the world thinks. Have you bought into it? Many Christian singles silently think that life without sex is asking too much of a single person. If we knew of all the illicit sexual relationships that take place within our Christian community, we'd be shocked. The world has infiltrated our thinking.

Not too long ago a young man started coming to our church and asking nice single women to go out with him. It's natural to think that if you cannot feel safe with someone you meet in church, who can you trust? But on the first date with these ladies, he would make an open proposition to go to bed. The word got out and some leaders took action. But I wonder how many young Christian women have succumbed to his allure. Though his approach was more forward than most, it's not uncommon for two Christian singles to find themselves overcome by their physical desires and going too far.

If you truly want to remain pure in your sexual life and keep yourself for the one person God has for you, or keep yourself for Christ if you remain single, you most certainly can do that. There is nothing impossible about it. It is a lie from Satan that tells us we can't live without sex.

However, in order to do that, you will need a discipline that I don't see in many singles. A discipline to go the extra mile in keeping the physical contact down to a minimum. You simply cannot trust the chemistry of your body. It is very powerful, and once it gets going, finding the discipline to keep it under control is extremely difficult. So the secret is to keep the electricity down to low levels by controlling the physical contact.

Watch where you put your hands. Watch the extremely

familiar poses, wrapping arms and legs around each other. It's great to be close and feel comfortable with each other, but you need to be aware that physical familiarity has to be carefully controlled or it will control you before you know it.

One very young woman wrote recently to say she and her boyfriend had ended up taking a shower together, and though they hadn't "gone all the way," she felt degraded. They had never intended to do it, she said, but it "just happened."

No, it didn't "just happen." First, it began when they were alone in the house; this gave them the opportunity. Then somehow they went from there to being alone in the bathroom, and next the shower—and so it goes. They put themselves into an environment that gave them the opportunity, and *then* it "just happened."

Let me tell you, it will "just happen" to most of us with that kind of temptation. When you think you "can handle it," when you assume that you know how far to go, when you believe that it would never happen to you, you're in trouble. The only cure here is prevention, and the only way you can prevent a sexual involvement with someone to whom you are attracted is to eliminate the opportunity.

In my thinking, that includes everyone at every age. You're never so old and mature that you've outgrown those temptations.

In 1 Corinthians 6:12–19, Paul gives us some very strong warnings about sexual immorality. First, he tells us that the body given to us by our Creator is not for the purpose of sexual immorality; it was given to us so that we could serve the Lord with it. That's where we have to start to correct our thinking, because this world age has led us to subconsciously believe that the reason we have bodies is for sexual fulfillment. *We're made for each other,* we think. No, we're made for God. Yes, God gave us sex to enhance and enrich our married lives, but that's not the primary reason we have bodies.

The Apostle then goes on to explain that we should "Flee from sexual immorality." Why? Because unlike other sins, sexual sins are committed against the body which was created for the Lord. Are you truly a Christian? If so, right now at this very moment the Holy Spirit of God dwells within that body you're wearing. Right there, right now. He doesn't stay home when you go on a date. You can't dismiss Him when you want to do what you want to do with your body.

So when we commit sexual sins and degrade our bodies, we drag the Holy Spirit of God through that ordeal. While sin is sin and all are evil, there is a special aspect to sexual sin which is particularly degrading to God's Spirit within us, and which is also very difficult to abandon, once you get started. That's why Paul tells us to flee from it.

Do you run from it, or do you see how far you can go? I've asked a friend of mine to let me share her story. I think it's a good illustration.

Amy (not her real name), now in her late thirties, received Christ as her Savior at ten years old and spent her teen years in a small town, where temptations were not as great as in other places. She was fortunate to have a strong local church with a very active youth group, where she learned biblical principles for dating and marriage clearly.

Amy took this teaching seriously and led a very circum-spect life.

She eventually attended Bible school and later joined a fine parachurch organization, working with high school students. She taught them the same things she had been taught about dating and marriage. Rather subtly, without realizing it, she began to develop a sense of pride about her pure life-style and her principled and disciplined attitude toward sex, dating, and marriage.

By her mid-thirties the reality of aging was setting in. Emotionally she still felt twenty-five, but her body was beginning to give strange messages—wrinkles, gray hair, and cellulite became real concerns! Maybe it was time, she thought, to consider her future marital status—soon. Some Christians she knew (and a lot more she'd heard about) had begun to listen to the world's view of premar-ital sex and had abandoned their earlier convictions. But not Amy. She was proud that she was still a faithful Christian.

She began working in downtown Chicago, where she was constantly bombarded with the yuppie life-style, which began to influence her own thinking toward their "you deserve to have it all" mind-set. She looked around and began comparing herself with others. She certainly was (and is) attractive, with a sparkling personality and good intelligence. "What's the problem, God?" became a frequent question for her.

She decided to give God a helping hand and wrote an ad for "Only Hearts," a personals column in a Chicago paper, designed to help singles meet each other. It was thirty-seven-lines long and gave the definite message that she was a "Miss Goody Two Shoes," which she figured would take care of any men with improper motives. She thought it would be a lot of fun, a bright spot in her routine life, and she was certain she could handle it.

After three ads and fifty-two responses, she had some material to choose from. None of these men were Christians, she learned, but she was quick to share her view on premarital sex with each one, and was rather proud that she could handle going out with non-Christian men.

But through all this she had slowly, bit by bit, stopped believing in God for His best for her life. She had taken the controls into her own hands, convinced that her strong principles would take her through this adventure which was like walking through a loaded minefield.

Later she joined a dating service and specifically requested Christian men. However, the prospects that came her way were disappointing to say the least—except for one. But he didn't call until nine months after she had canceled her membership, and he was not a Christian.

At first they met "just for coffee." His voice on the phone was attractive, but in person he was even more appealing. The conversation was enjoyable, he showed signs of thoughtfulness (not easy to find), and they agreed to have dinner together.

After dinner, they took a lovely walk by Chicago's lakefront, and the romantic setting was all in place. First there were touches, nothing really overt, but definitely sexual. She did tell him at that time that she didn't believe in premarital sex, and he, in an incredulous tone of voice, said, "But . . . you've never been married!" "That's right," Amy said, and as they said good night, she was again proud that she could handle going out with a sexy non-Christian man and come out unscathed.

But, of course, that wasn't the end. He called again, which was flattering to Amy, and they agreed to meet. Amy convinced herself this was all legitimate and above-board because she was using every opportunity she could to tell him about her faith in Christ. But she soon discovered that you can't put yourself in the middle of temptation and then use testifying as a rationalization for doing what you know you shouldn't do.

Their next evening together was even lovelier, the setting more romantic, and his warm arm on a chilly evening got gently warmer as the night went on. As Amy describes it, "I didn't know it then, but I was 'walking into the enemy's camp, laying my weapons down, shedding my armor as I went, and leaving it on the ground.' "

After a lovely concert in the park, followed by another romantic walk, the physical fire was lit. He pulled her over and this strong, protective, virile man wrapped his arms around her and gently moved his lips toward hers. It was no casual kiss; the sparks flew, and they both knew it. Another kiss ended that evening together, but left a strong desire for more.

The next night they went bike riding together. Familiar touches seemed to just happen, and that enticing kiss was much easier to give in to now. Finally, late that evening, they were putting her bike away in her building's bike room. It was a quiet, secluded room, and before she knew it, the gentle kisses were passionate and their emotions were out of control, as well as their caresses. He asked to go up to her apartment, which she refused, saying she did not intend to go to bed with him. But all the while her actions in the bike room were sending another message entirely.

"I will always remember that moment," says Amy. "The Holy Spirit stepped in and whispered to my heart, 'That's enough. I won't let you go any further.' My eyes were opened to the sin I'd just committed. I looked up at my date and said, 'We don't love each other; I hardly even know you. This was something I was saving for my husband on my wedding night. I've never let a man touch my breasts. And now I won't have that gift to give my husband. I'm sorry I let this happen—for your sake and mine.' "

He must have realized the impact on Amy, because he dropped his arms and moved away at once. He offered to talk about it later, but Amy told him they didn't need to talk anymore, they both knew where the other one stood—on sex and on Jesus Christ.

Amy went up to her apartment to deal with the aftermath of what had happened. She felt sick—sick to realize the potential for sin that resided in her. And all these years she had felt so pure! Having become a Christian at ten years old, she didn't have a dramatic before-and-after experience, and without realizing it, she had seen herself as better than other Christians—her sins weren't really all that bad.

Now she experienced what it meant to grieve the Holy Spirit with her sin. She said, "When I get to heaven and talk to Eve, I think I'll have a better understanding of what she went through. We both had a problem with pride, thinking we knew better than God what was best for us."

That was a long night for Amy. She couldn't face her sixth-grade Sunday school students the next morning. The healing wasn't over, and in a sense, it still isn't. Through willful disobedience and by not running away from temptation, she allowed herself to be scarred by sin, and one of those scars, she says, is sensual lust. "God had given me a gift for thirty-eight years and I didn't even know it. That night I forfeited the gift. My mind and emotions were awakened to a temptation I'd never experienced before. Believe it or not, God had allowed me to go all those years without experiencing sensual lust. He protected me as I was obedient to Him, in spite of my pride. I was disobedient to His laws, and now I'm paying the price. Yes, He forgave me, and the sin is paid for; but I must face the consequences.

"God is slowly healing that scar, leaving just enough so that when people ask me how I got it, I can warn them— so they won't have to go through the pain I did. If God has given you the gift of freedom from sensual lust, don't forfeit it for the counterfeit 'gifts' the world has to offer."

Unfortunately, unlike Amy there are very few single people who reach their thirties without experiencing sensual lust. Our society promotes it at every turn, and I'm sure that even some of the people reading this now think Amy is an anachronism—perhaps even warped in some way—never to have experienced sexual lust, or to have allowed a physical relationship to go that far until then.

That's because we have been infiltrated with the world's view, to the point that purity of thought and life is considered a joke, something possible only for weird people who don't live in the real world. That's a satanic lie, and our enemy has sure done a good job of putting that one over on us!

Yet, I ask you to consider the results of this lie. Does sexual permissiveness buy anything more than temporary relief from sensual lust? Do we see in our society any sign that it has brought any kind of social good to people? Are marriages more stable? Are people less paranoid? Can you find any statistics to show that we've made progress through our permissive attitude toward sex?

No, quite the opposite. There are many hard facts to substantiate the truth of God — sex outside the bonds of marriage is not only immoral, it is the pathway to personal destruction, both physical and emotional.

Perhaps, even if just for a few people, Amy's story will help get our thinking back into biblical molds.

Mistake: We think that the only necessary requirement for a date or mate is that he or she is a Christian.

I don't believe that there is only one person in this whole world whom God intends for us to marry, and if we miss that person, we've missed our perfect mate. (Of course, I don't believe that it's necessarily true that each of us is intended by God to be married. But that's another subject!) I think it's possible to find more than one person with whom you can be compatible and have a good lifelong relationship.

However, there's more to those prerequisites than simply looking for someone who is a Christian. When I was a teenager, that was the thinking that I picked up: If I date only Christian boys, I'll marry a Christian boy, and everything will be happy ever after. *Wrong!*

I can think of a few Christian couples, in which both partners were committed Christians, who have been counseled out of marrying each other by their pastors because they recognized significant potential incompatibility.

I also can think of a couple who seemed very incompatible to one of our pastors, and he gave them careful warning. They thought it through and did eventually marry. Their relationship improves all the time, and they're doing fine, though they admit it hasn't been easy. But they were made aware of the potential problems, and they entered marriage prepared to work at solving them.

Our pastoral staff has decided in the past few years to strengthen the counseling given to engaged couples and to hold to even stricter standards before agreeing to marry a couple. Our society makes it very easy to get married. Of all the critical decisions we make in life, this one is the most emotional and the easiest to make. Career decisions take much more time and require more qualifying.

It's very smart to put yourself through intensive soul-searching when you consider marrying someone. Keeping in mind that your emotions are involved and therefore your perspective may be off center, ask for advice from trusted people. Get them to play devil's advocate and throw every question they can at you. Take every compatibility test you can find. Do all you can do to know what you're getting into before you jump. You'll never be totally prepared for marriage, but it's a good idea to try to find out before you walk down the aisle whether or not this match is likely to work well.

I mentioned a friend who married a man against everyone's best judgment. She was determined to marry him, but I believe she's paying a high price for it now. If your friends and family are not excited about your relationship with a person, check it out. They may be seeing something you can't see. If it's the right relationship, close scrutiny won't destroy it.

Mistake: We carry our list of requirements for a relationship with us and judge others too quickly and selfishly.

I used to have a list of the things I wanted in a man. The list was divided into "Essential" and "Nonessential." Now, that's not an altogether bad idea. My best friends, Fran and Dick, have a beautiful forty-year marriage, and Fran had her list before Dick came along. She decided very early what the man she married must be and it was helpful in her decision process.

My "Essential" list now has one thing on it: "Must be someone who would enhance my walk with God and allow us to have a more effective ministry together than we have separately." By that priority, I have probably eliminated marriage from my future, but I'm in a different stage of life than many of you reading this book. If you're younger, you have other legitimate desires that would give you a different perspective.

Isn't it great that our God is big enough to deal with all our differences and idiosyncrasies. He isn't looking for "cookie-cutter Christians," all of us looking and acting just alike in every way. We certainly all have the same biblical principles to apply to our lives, but within those principles, there's much room for individuality and personality. Amen to that!

Many singles, however, seem to have a long list of requirements for their potential date or mate, and they've gotten a bit carried away with it, probably as a reaction to the many failed marriages around us. It's as though they're checking you out, making sure you meet their needs. They approach this area of their lives as they might approach buying a car: What features do you have and what are the benefits of those features to me?

In one of my focus groups, a young man related how he had gotten carried away with his checklist and it backfired on him. He met a young woman who checked off very nicely. She met all his requirements, so he figured she was the one. After a short engagement, they discovered this was not the perfect match made in heaven and broke the engagement.

One thing he felt he had learned through this experience was that he had approached the relationship, selfishly asking, "What can you do for me?" instead of bringing a perspective of "How can I meet your needs and help you?"

Again, we have to look for balance in this area. Having certain important guidelines in mind as we meet and date people is helpful in keeping us from making totally emotional decisions. But checking people out for selfish reasons is going too far.

Mistake: We think that anything is better than being alone.

While it's true that we have basic needs for companionship, it's not true that aloneness is the worst condition in the whole world. Note that I said *aloneness,* not *loneliness.* There's a big difference, you know.

I am alone much of the time, because I live alone. Many singles are not alone much at all, because they live with others and are on the go all the time. But whether or not you're alone, you can still be lonely. Loneliness is an attitude; aloneness is a circumstance.

Most people fear aloneness because to them it represents loneliness. They haven't learned to fill their time so that aloneness is valuable and refreshing for them. I have learned to love my aloneness, but it has not always been that way. It has come as I've learned to enjoy the presence of God and stopped equating aloneness with loneliness.

I used to think that a Saturday night alone was a fate worse than death. In my thinking, if you didn't have something interesting to do on a Saturday night, something was really wrong with you. That was "date night" to me, so it was very important to have a date for Saturday night. Now, that didn't always happen, but then I would plan some other social function to take the place of the date I really wanted, if necessary. Anything to keep busy and not be alone on Saturday night. I have a feeling many of you can relate to that.

Even after I came back to God and committed my whole life to His control, that feeling didn't change overnight. One Wednesday, I was sitting in my office and I realized I had no plans for the coming weekend. It was like a panic attack, and my immediate reaction was to reach for the phone and start calling a few friends to make some plans. As I dialed the first number, that inner voice I was learning to hear said so clearly, "Can't you trust Me? Don't you know I am God of the weekends, too?"

I put the phone down and gulped. When the Spirit of God speaks to you so directly, you're pinned against the wall, and it wasn't comfortable right at that moment. *God of the weekends, too,* I thought. *Oh, sure, but I still don't want to be alone on Saturday night.* After a few minutes of vacillation, I said, "Okay, Lord, I'll not make any plans for this weekend, and I'll plan time with You for Saturday night. I'll prove that You are God of the weekends."

Things went great that weekend, and I accomplished a lot. I had planned to do some good reading Saturday evening and spend some of that time in prayer. No problem, until about 9:00 P.M. Then panic started to hit again. *I'm alone on Saturday evening. What's wrong with me?* There was that attitude creeping back into my thinking, and no wonder. It had been there for years, so cleaning it out was bound to take a bit of time.

What did I do? I just told the Lord how I felt. I cried, "Help," and He rescued me. Have you learned to yell for help to the Lord at those panic moments? David did it all the time, and we need to do the same thing. Here are a few examples:

> In my distress I called to the Lord; I cried to God for help. . . .
>
> Psalm 18:6

> O Lord my God, I called to you for help and you healed me.
>
> Psalm 30:2

> This poor man called, and the Lord heard him; he saved him out of all his troubles.
>
> Psalm 34:6

There's no question that we all have moments of loneliness, whether we're married or single. A letter from one mother said, "I am a Christian, but still have feelings of loneliness even though I am surrounded by a husband and four sons." Sometimes the loneliest place in the world is right in the middle of a crowd.

Loneliness is a feeling, an attitude. We don't get through this life without experiencing it to some degree. But to settle for *anything* as a substitute for loneliness is a big mistake. There are worse things than loneliness, and by God's grace we do not have to be overcome and defeated by loneliness. He can take our aloneness and turn it into beautiful, fruitful, productive time with Him.

Take it from one who knows what she's talking about. Learn the wonderful secret of enjoying your aloneness. It saves you so much grief. Recognize that being alone doesn't mean you're a social misfit. Don't buy into the lies of our enemy who wants you to feel desperate. When we feel desperate, we act in irrational and unprincipled ways. When we feel an overpowering need to have someone near, we'll settle for anything.

Also recognize your need for social interaction and plan good things. I invited a young couple who are my good friends over for hamburgers this weekend because, as I said to Julie, "I haven't seen you two in so long, and besides, I've been by myself too much lately." It's not good to be alone too much; you can become too introspective. But you don't have to have a date to have company; reach out to others and share your time. Not with the idea that it's second best, you'd rather have a date but since you can't, you'll be with friends. Enjoy those people for who they are, and you'll discover that the loneliness goes away.

3

Common Mistakes Women Make in Relationships With Males

"Since there are so few sharp Christian men, when we meet someone who is, we tend to think this is 'the one' and either settle for second best (i.e., we know deep down inside this is not the right guy for us—though he is neat and has a lot going for him), or we scare that guy away by being too anxious and overly enthusiastic. . . . God knows what is best and life is a lot more fulfilling when we follow his game plan and not ours. He is not an ogre trying to deprive us of things."

"My sister-in-law is having trouble in her life right now. . . . She is thirty-five years old and has never been married, but she falls too easily for men, then gets hurt."

"I met a guy at church about one and a half years ago. We've really grown a lot together. We are really good friends, but it has gotten to the point where I truly love him. . . . The only problem is he's kind of quiet about how he feels. . . . I've wanted to talk to him about this for a long time, but as talkative, aggressive, and bold as I am, I'm

afraid to bring our feelings up. . . . I'm afraid that if we bring up how we feel and he doesn't feel the same, I'll lose our friendship."

* * *

Can you hear yourself in some of these words? They are typical examples of letters from single women who are struggling with relating to men or to a man.

In looking at mistakes in relationships with the opposite sex, I found there were some that were unique to each sex. So, this chapter looks at mistakes women tend to make, and the next one deals with those of the men.

Mistake: We panic over the scarcity of Christian men.

Here's a verse that every single woman wishes were her life verse:

> Be merciful to me, O God, for men hotly pursue me; all day long they press their attack.
>
> Psalm 56:1

However, the single's version would read: "Be merciful to me, O God, *and let* men hotly pursue me"!

There's no question that we have this urge to find a lifelong relationship. It's born in us. We want a commitment from that one special man, and those natural urges are very strong.

But here's a verse we single women should memorize:

Many a man claims to have unfailing love, but a faithful man who can find?

Proverbs 20:6

How many times have single women said to me something like this: "Where can you find a really sharp Christian man?" I admit, it's not easy. I'm sure men think it's not easy to find just the woman they want, either, but it's no secret that there are usually more women than men involved in church and Christian groups. That's true in every category—young, old, single, or married. It's also true that there are more women than men in this world. So, add those two facts up, and you have a shortage of single Christian men—not enough to go around.

I've often pondered why there seem to be more committed Christian women than men. Kari Malcolm, author of *Women at the Crossroads*, gave me a good explanation a few years ago. She pointed out that people who are depressed in any way turn to God more readily. You see this in different countries and cultures. The most depressed people with the fewest possessions, rights, luxuries, or the least freedom seem much more willing to make a firm commitment of their life to Christ.

Because women have been treated in some ways as second-class citizens, we certainly have had a more deprived environment as a whole, with less opportunities and options open to us. That deprivation has probably been a key reason women have been more willing to follow Jesus Christ. In other words, we're needier—or rather, we recognize our need more readily—than men. And that's always the starting place for knowing God.

When we think we can get by on our own without much trouble, we aren't as likely to seek the Lord.

I see that changing, as women's attitudes are affected by the new equality and opportunities available to us. I would like to think that we're smart enough not to throw the baby out with the bathwater, but my instincts tell me that's probably not the case. As we get rid of the unfair treatment, we're likely to lose that vulnerableness and openness to things of God which characterized us in the past.

At any rate, faced with a shortage of "sharp Christian men," we must learn to live with it and not allow ourselves to go nuts over any Christian man who comes along, nor allow ourselves to be plunged into despair. I know one single woman who pounces on every new single man who walks into the singles group. I guess she wants to get there first, since the pickings are slim.

Have more respect for who you are as a child of God than to let yourself get caught in that trap. If you've constantly got your radar working, allowing the "man-hunt" to occupy all your thinking, it's a sign that you are not really trusting God. A few probing questions here:

What is your first thought when you see or meet a new Christian man? Let me guess: *Is he single?* If you know he's single, your first thought may be, *Is he taken?* Now, I don't know if you'll ever be able to stop that first thought (I find it still happens to me on occasions), but the secret here is to immediately abandon that line of thinking. Say to yourself, "This is first of all a person, not a man. I will relate to him as I would to any new person I was meeting.

I will not allow myself to look at him as a potential partner."

Do you care about Christian single men who are not attractive to you? Do you still care about them as fellow believers, and try to reach out to them as you can? Or do you view all single men in two categories, potential and no-potential? That's wrong thinking, for women and men. We need to ask God to help us see each man as a person, with strengths and weaknesses, problems and joys, who may just need a Christian friend.

Do you find you are feeling sorry for yourself or commiserating with other single women about the shortage of men? I frequently hear talk like this among single women. It's not a great topic for conversation, for you simply keep reinforcing the idea that there's a big problem finding a Christian man, and that starts affecting your thinking. It causes depression and dreariness. I see it on the faces of single women so often—the look that says, "Oh, poor me, I'm a good Christian woman, but where are the Christian men?"

It's one thing to recognize the shortage. It's another thing to let that reality control and depress you. That's the same as saying, "God, You're helpless in view of the fact that there aren't enough Christian men to go around, so I have no choice but to be hopeless." Either God is sovereign, or He's no better than the wooden idols worshiped by pagan religions. If He is truly the God described in Scripture, and we truly believe that He is, then we can't hold on to that attitude of depression just because things aren't exactly the way we think they should be. Isaiah 40:22 tells us that our God "sits enthroned above the circle of the earth, and its people are like grasshoppers." God is in control of the number of men and women there are in this world, and He's in control of what happens to you.

I have discovered that when I'm having difficulty accepting some situation, it goes back to my lack of trust in the sovereign God. When you really focus on believing that God is in control, it changes your outlook on the circumstances of your life. You *have* to trust Him; nothing else makes sense.

So, if you've been depressed or worried or desperate because of the lack of "sharp Christian men," please spend some time getting to know the sovereignty of God. That's the cure. Read Isaiah 40 and 50. They are great reminders of God's sovereignty; so live in those chapters for a few days.

Remember the basic truth that God has good plans for you. He intends to bring joy and contentment into your life. And He has many ways to do that; He's not limited to one method for us. We limit Him. We think: *Lord, I must have a Christian man in my life. That's where it's at, Lord! Please send me that man!* I know it's difficult, but please believe that God has other ways and means of blessing you and fulfilling you.

I receive many letters each month from women asking me to pray that God will send them Christian husbands. I find it difficult to just pray, "God, she needs a Christian husband. Please send."

But what I can and do pray is that God will work in them His goodwill. I pray that they would be conformed to the image of Jesus Christ, and that if marriage is in God's plan for them, they will have wisdom and discernment in making that decision, and in the meantime God would be preparing them for each other. It's the same prayer I've prayed for myself, and most recently, for my daughter, Julie, who was just married to the man God prepared for her.

Do you see the difference in those two prayers? In the first instance, we are deciding for God what we know to be best for us, and asking Him to please deliver, soon! In the second, we are admitting our desires and needs, telling Him we want a Christian husband, but allowing Him to make the decision.

Most single women don't believe that God can truly make us fulfilled and happy except through marriage. There are some problems with that kind of mind-set. First of all, it assumes that God *owes* us happiness and fulfillment. I can't find that in Scripture. He has promised us joy and peace and contentment, and when you have those, happiness and fulfillment are often by-products. But not always.

When I think of the most godly people I know, I see that their lives have not been one happy event after another, with everything fulfilling and exciting. But through all their circumstances, happy or not, they have had peace and joy and abiding contentment. When you have these three things, nothing else really matters. Very few people in this world know anything at all about peace and contentment, and sadly, Christians often don't seem to have much of it either.

Again, we keep putting the cart before the horse. We

don't find fulfillment by filling up our lives with things
that we think will make us happy, such as a man. We find
fulfillment when we stop looking for it and concentrate
instead on knowing God. Look at what the Apostle Paul
says we need to be filled with (the italics are mine):

> And I pray that you, being rooted and established in love,
> may have power, together with all the saints, to grasp
> how wide and long and high and deep is the love of
> Christ, and to know this love that surpasses knowledge —
> that you may be *filled to the measure of all the fullness of God.*
>
> Ephesians 3:17–19

> . . . be *filled with the Spirit.*
>
> Ephesians 5:18

> And this is my prayer: that your love may abound more
> and more in knowledge and depth of insight, so that you
> may be able to discern what is best and may be pure and
> blameless until the day of Christ, *filled with the fruit of
> righteousness* that comes through Jesus Christ — to the
> glory and praise of God.
>
> Philippians 1:9–11

> For this reason, since the day we heard about you, we
> have not stopped praying for you and asking God *to fill
> you with the knowledge of his will* through all spiritual
> wisdom and understanding.
>
> Colossians 1:9

Fulfillment comes when we are filled with the fullness
of God, filled with the Spirit, filled with the fruit of

righteousness that comes through Jesus, filled with the knowledge of God's will. This is how Paul prayed for the people he loved, and this is how we should pray for ourselves.

Second, when we insist that marriage is essential to our lives, we show that we think we're smarter than God. We know what will make us happy, and we don't want God or anyone else changing the game plan. Isaiah 48:17, 18 says: "This is what the Lord says—your Redeemer, the Holy One of Israel: 'I am the Lord your God, who teaches you what is best for you, who directs you in the way you should go. If only you had paid attention to my commands, your peace would have been like a river, your righteousness like the waves of the sea.' "

The "if onlys" of our lives are sad. When we get to heaven, will we hear God say, "If only you had relinquished control to Me, I had something so good planned for you, but I couldn't deliver because you thought you knew better than I"? I don't want any "if onlys" from God. I want to hear, "You finished what I gave you to do," just as He told Jesus at the end of His earthly life. I want to hear, "Well done, good and faithful servant."

Third, insisting that we have to be married demonstrates that we don't trust God. It shows we don't understand that He's a God of love, planning only what is good for us. We're afraid to trust Him because who knows what He might do. He might never send us a Christian man—heaven forbid!

One of my favorite verses is Jeremiah 29:11: " 'For I know the plans I have for you,' declares the Lord, 'plans to prosper you and not to harm you, plans to give you hope and a future.' " Memorize that verse so you can easily quote it to yourself when you start to think that the future is bleak because there aren't enough Christian men to go around. God has good plans for you, with or without a Christian man.

Two verses later, we read " 'You will seek me and find me when you seek me with all your heart. I will be found by you,' declares the Lord. . . ." There's that secret again—focusing our lives on seeking God with all our hearts.

You can know a totally fulfilling life when your life is filled up with Jesus Christ. He has promised us life abundant, and that's exactly what He has for you. You may be missing it altogether because you're looking for it in one place—a Christian man—and the Lord wants to deliver through another avenue.

How often have I missed a blessing God had for me because I was dictating the terms to God, while He was trying to get me to see He had a better idea? If your mind is focused on the shortage of Christian men, you may well miss the good things God's waiting to give you, because you're looking in the wrong place.

The scarcity of Christian men is not your major problem. Your major problem, and mine, is learning to trust God in every area of our lives. Most of our frustrations can be traced to our poor understanding of who God is, and to our failure to trust Him completely. In my own life, I can see it at every turn: The more I know about God, the more I trust Him. The more I trust Him, the less I worry—about men or anything else. And the less I worry, the more I am contented and joyful and filled with the fullness of Jesus Christ.

But as soon as I get away from that focus, and fail to seek God with my whole heart, as sure as day follows night, depression, discouragement, self-pity, hopelessness start walking in the door, robbing me of contentment and peace.

It's not worth it! Please don't be fearful about the scarcity of "sharp Christian men." If you're not careful, that fear will start to control your thinking, and thereby your life.

Mistake: We think and talk too much about men.

Recently while in the New York area, I had dinner with one of my single listeners, a young woman who is seeking with all her heart to follow Christ and is having a real impact on her world. She is obsessed with being the woman God wants her to be. Like most single women, she hopes to be married someday, but recognizes that God may have other options and allows Him that control.

She commented that when she is with her single Christian girlfriends, the first, and frequently only, topic of conversation seems to be men. After a recent Bible study and prayer time, as she left with some single female friends, the first things they said were, "Did you see any men there you really liked?" "Which one do you like best?"

She said, "I wasn't thinking about the eligibility of the

men in the group, and I almost felt foolish saying to my friends, 'Well, I really didn't think about it.' "

Her friends' response was one of disbelief: "Oh, come on, we know better. Tell us the truth; which one do you like?" The attitude was that any normal woman would be thinking about the eligible men, and to claim anything else was hypocritical or abnormal, or both.

We women perpetuate this type of attitude because we allow ourselves to think about men too much and we talk with each other about them too much. Am I being "superspiritual" to suggest that a normal single Christian woman could think and talk about other things and have other priorities? Couldn't we help to build each other up and encourage each other by talking about spiritual truths, how they apply to our lives? Wouldn't it be refreshing to come away from a time with women friends without even having mentioned men?

By allowing conversations about men to occupy our time together, we keep inflicting on each other this mentality that without a man we're not complete. It's bad enough to have society inflict that on us at every turn; do we have to do it to ourselves?

Of course, there's nothing wrong with that topic coming up occasionally, since that is a part of our lives. But I'm referring to the obsessiveness that is altogether too evident in our "girl talk"—and of course, in our "girl thinking" as well.

Start listening to your female conversations a little more carefully. Try to steer them away from the topic of men. Not only will you find it refreshing to talk about something else, but you'll also be changing your thinking. We talk about what we think about and we think about what we talk about. And we are what we think. How I pray that some of you reading this will make a real effort to change this tendency and not keep making this mistake.

Mistake: We're afraid to share our real feelings with men or express our opinions.

I've seen this trait in women both in personal and business relationships with men. We often seem to have a reluctance to say what we really think. I think this fear has several possible sources:

1. We're not really sure if what we have to say is valid. We fear we may show our ignorance by expressing our thoughts openly. We lack confidence in our experience or opinions.
2. We're intimidated by a male presence. Many women just clam up when a man's around.
3. We don't want to come on too strong, because we've learned that many men have difficulty dealing with women who have their own ideas and opinions.
4. In a personal relationship, we fear losing the man if we express our feelings and he doesn't like what he hears.

Well, whatever the cause of our reluctance to express our ideas, we need to remember that God didn't give men better minds and intellects than He gave us. Galatians 3:28 reminds us that there is neither male nor female with God, for we are all one in Christ. It is not right for us to be fearful of expressing ourselves simply because we are women.

Now, all of us should be very careful about what we say and how we say it. God certainly doesn't give us the right to use words carelessly. But when we have thoughtful ideas and opinions, we should not hesitate to express them.

If you've been struggling with this, perhaps you can pinpoint the reason behind your reluctance and start praying about it. Ask God to give you a balanced view, where you guard your words carefully but at the same time, you don't cower in a corner, fearful to speak simply because you're a woman talking to a man.

If expressing your feelings might destroy the relationship, then it was fairly fragile to begin with. It might not be worth saving. One of the key ingredients to any healthy relationship is to know that you can express your real feelings and not be blasted out of the saddle for it.

Mistake: We tend to be too open, too vulnerable, too transparent.

One of the things I love about women is that we tend to be open and transparent. To me, it is so refreshing to meet and talk with someone who simply is "up front," without pretense, with whom it doesn't take two years to dig under the skin and find out what's really inside. So, it's not easy for me to identify this as a mistake.

I suppose if you had to find one word to describe me, it might be *open.* I guess that's why I love this trait so much in others. I also know that openness helps people communicate better; it helps us reach out to other people. I can't tell you how often someone says to me, "When you shared how you felt, I could really relate," or, "Because you're so honest about your feelings, it gives me hope."

Well, that's how God has made me, and I praise Him that He uses the personality traits He gives to us. It's no mistake that I'm an open person. But I also know that every personality trait can have a dark side. It's possible to take anything too far, and it's very possible to be too open and too transparent.

I know because, as you can guess, I've done it many times. But after a few years of sticking my feet in my mouth and making a fool out of myself, I'm learning that it is prudent to keep this tendency under control.

In relationships with men, I've been too willing to tell just how I feel far too soon. My rationalization was, "If he really gets to know me, and sees just how I feel about him, how can he possibly resist my honesty and openness." I just assumed that men appreciated transparency as much as I did.

I started to wake up when one man said to me, "Mary, I'll never be as open as you are. I wish I could, but it won't happen." As I look back on that relationship, I recognize that I probably frightened him or at least made him very uncomfortable by being so totally open myself. Yet, at the time, I thought it was honest and smart and admirable on my part to be this totally open person.

Please understand that I'm not advocating deception or dishonesty here. But wisdom will teach us not to say everything we think, not to express all our feelings.

Proverbs 15:23 says, "A man [or woman] finds joy in giving an apt reply—and how good is a timely word!" And again in Proverbs 17:27: "A man [or woman] of knowledge uses words with restraint, and a man of understanding is even-tempered."

I don't believe that guarding our words and suppressing our desire to say everything we feel is "playing games." I recognize that playing games is not acceptable behavior, when we are trying to manipulate people or events for our benefit. But an overreaction to that style could lead us to use words without restraint and speak words that are not timely.

Pray for balance! I think I've said that before, haven't I? Well, truly it should be a constant prayer we lay before the Lord, to give us balance in these areas, so that we are not at one extreme or the other.

Well, good news—that's the end of mistakes women make toward men! Now the women can enjoy the next chapter, where I give men equal time.

4

Common Mistakes Men Make in Relationships With Females

"I don't think a lot is out in the open (in relationships with women). I think men talk less than women."

"I think women tend to be willing to open themselves up, while society dictates that men have to be secure and strong and less emotional than women. Women aren't raised that way, so women share the time they've had, but men only share in a bragging mode."

"Singles in the church hang on to the stereotypes that the church had. Society has lost their stereotype for a particular gender, but I don't think the evangelical community has. There's a church ideal versus a society ideal, and that creates a tension for Christian singles."

* * *

Above are some comments made by men in my focus groups. Insightful and candid analysis, I think.

I confess that I was more comfortable writing chapter 3 on the mistakes of women than I am with this chapter, which focuses on the mistakes men make. But I think perhaps I have a perspective, based on many years of observing and participating in the "singles scene," which might be helpful to my male readers, so I'll take the risk.

Mistake: Men are too visually oriented and don't give themselves a chance to know a woman who doesn't meet their visual ideal.

It seems to be a physiological fact that men respond to visual stimuli much more than women do, and women respond to verbal stimuli more than men do. That has given rise to the notion that a woman can be sweet-talked into anything, and sometimes that's true. But it's also true that an overemphasis on visual input has many dangers.

I have discovered that many men have a stronger idea of what they want in the physical appearance of a woman than of what they want in her character or personality. I've asked my dear friend Rick if I can use him as an example. Rick is a good-looking single man in his early thirties. We've been friends for a few years, and in the course of that friendship have shared many conversations about what he likes in a woman.

One of the first things he told me was that he really preferred a brunette over a blonde. Well, I'm certain he's sorry he ever told me that, for I've teased him many times about wanting to introduce him to a terrific woman, but unfortunately she was blonde! He also has mentioned certain other physical characteristics that were important to him.

Because Rick is very serious about his relationship with

Jesus Christ, his attitude has changed. While a woman's looks are not something he now ignores (and I'm sure his head still turns faster for a brunette), he recognizes the unfairness of holding such artificial qualifications for a future mate and the lack of trust that demonstrates in God. So, he sings a different tune these days.

For some men, it is shape or size that is most important. For others it's hair or skin. But most men, if honest, would admit that they really place a high importance on some aspect of a woman's physical appearance.

I'm not proposing that men should miraculously change their physiological makeup and dismiss appearance as a nonessential, but I am suggesting that this tendency can easily get out of hand, and a Christian man needs to check it out. "Looks don't last, cookin' do," the old adage goes, and there's something there to think about.

The qualities that make a relationship meaningful and durable are not found in a person's looks. Yet many single men simply refuse to associate with or get to know a woman at all unless she visually meets their standards. You may pass up a terrific woman by refusing to get to know her just because she's not exactly what you were dreaming of.

Have you ever thought about the underlying reason a man wants a woman who's a "knockout" by his visual standards? Part of it undoubtedly must be that it simply pleases him visually, but could it not also be an ego trip? Could it be you men want to have a woman who creates a dynamite impression on others, so when people see her they say, "Wow"? And if you're with a "Wow" woman, what does that make you? It elevates your value and your stature as a man to have a "doll" on your arm, doesn't it?

And that puts us right in the middle of a problem identified in Scripture as pride.

I didn't realize until I had come back to God and was walking closely with Him that during my desperate years when I was looking for "Mr. Right," my motivation for finding this wonderful man was very suspect. While I didn't have standards based on physical appearance, I had qualifications based on sophistication and "presence," as I called it. Clearly and gently God showed me one day that what I had been looking for was not the right man that God had for me, but a man I could wear like a badge. With that man, people would say, "Wow, Mary must be something special to get a man like that!"

Can you read between those lines? Pride certainly reeks through every word. I wanted to appear to be somebody; I wanted people to envy me. Selfishness is apparent, for I cared about what he could do for me, not what I could bring to him. I also had a severe misunderstanding of what makes a person valuable and what brings significance to one's existence. And by the way, I was a Christian at that time.

It might be a good idea to check out the motivations behind your desire for the girl who meets your visual requirements. They could be quite sinful and/or inappropriate.

Mistake: Men have difficulty expressing their feelings and are afraid of losing their "manly" image by showing too much emotion.

The men who discussed this in one of my focus groups felt that this difficulty is both cultural and innate. Certainly I think we can all agree that traditionally we have cultivated the image of the "strong" man who never admits to his feelings. How many mothers have said to their little boys, "Big boys don't cry"? How many fathers have refused to show outward affection to their sons because "boys don't kiss"?

But I see that changing in the younger generations, and I'm glad for that change. Meanwhile, those in older age categories struggle with the leftover impressions.

I think the best thing I could say on this subject is to tell my male readers that for most women two of the most appealing characteristics in a man are gentleness and compassion, and both of those have a lot to do with showing your feelings. For me, the gentleness of Jesus Christ is the most alluring and winsome aspect of His manhood. Think about Jesus: He touched people—physically touched them. He cried over a city and He cried when a dear friend died. He cared about the physical needs of people He loved. Think of how He expressed His own feelings and needs to His friends in the Garden of Gethsemane.

It's no wonder women followed Him everywhere, taking care of His needs, contributing to His ministry, and standing at the foot of the cross in large numbers. If you need a role model, you have one in Jesus Christ. He treated women with such great respect—and ever so gently, showing His feelings and showing compassion.

The more you get to know Him, whether male or female, the more vulnerable you become because you're more like Jesus. It seems to me that Christian men should be able to exhibit appropriate levels of feelings and compassion, even if it's a new experience. Getting to know Jesus would produce that kind of relationship with others.

Jesus came to make us into new creations; "the old has gone, the new has come," we read in 2 Corinthians 5:17. Therefore, those personality traits or characteristics that we've carried around with us for a long time can be changed, if it's to the honor and glory of Jesus Christ. I believe that if Christian men who sensed they needed to be more open and able to express their feelings would pray for that ability and spend time getting to know Jesus, it would happen.

I mentioned in the last chapter that I am a very open person, and most women do tend to be more open than men. Remember that man in my life a few years ago who said quite candidly to me, "Mary, I'll never be as open as you are. I just can't do it." I can agree with him in two respects: One, I'm extremely open and that might be asking too much of any man. And two, without the power of Jesus Christ in one's life, it's difficult if not impossible to change those basic qualities ingrained in us from birth. My friend didn't know Christ, so he's probably right—he just can't do it.

There is no male romantic relationship in my life at this point, but I observe relationships very carefully. I have noticed that in good marriages although the wife may be better at expressing her feelings, the man has learned to do so also.

As I mentioned in the introduction, I conducted some focus group discussions before writing this book, and one group was for men only. That was an interesting evening! And I must say that those men talked freely.

However, my observation was that they talked in third person much more than the female groups did. They talked theory and philosophy very easily, but personal experience came more hesitatingly and carefully. I don't think we can expect to see any dramatic swings in that tendency. Perhaps it wouldn't even be good if that were to happen, but I would hope more and more Christian men begin to see the benefit of expressing their real feelings a bit more freely, and feel confident enough in Christ to let that happen.

Mistake: Men are frightened of a lifetime commitment.

One message that came through loud and clear in my focus groups was the big difference between men and women in their attitude toward a lifetime commitment. The women were focused on "Will it happen?" and "Where is he?" The men were just as anxious to find that right person, just as ready to admit they wanted it, but much more cautious about making any moves.

What causes their reluctance and fear? Here are some suggestions:

Fear of rejection. I've long realized that men want to be fairly certain they're not going to get hurt before they take a risk on a relationship. Women are ready for any risks!

We women look at the male role with envy. The men have the ball in their court; if they see a woman who is attractive to them, all they have to do is pick up the phone and make the first move. We have to sit back and hope. The men have a different view of that role. They are the ones on the spot when they do make a move, and rejection is a difficult blow to deal with.

Fear of failure.   The men seemed to be more aware of the failed marriages and the aftermath of that failure. They were more concerned about the possibility of making a wrong choice and the results of that wrong decision.

Fear of the responsibilities of marriage.   These days there seems to be much more awareness among men of the financial responsibilities that marriage brings, and a reluctance to take on those responsibilities too quickly. I think this new awareness is mostly helpful, but let me hasten to say you'll probably never feel totally comfortable about handling those responsibilities. It's always a little scary. If you're waiting for a feeling of total security about finances before making any moves, it may never come! Of course, that drives us back to God, doesn't it? All our insecurities and inabilities to handle everything ourselves should have the positive effect of bringing us to our knees and looking to our only true source, our heavenly Father.

Men want to keep their options open.   Perhaps some of the reason for this reluctance to make a lifetime commitment is the thought that something better might yet come along.

If this fear of commitment is something you've been struggling with, I would remind you that any fear we have is always from our enemy, Satan, because God has not given us the spirit of fear (2 Timothy 1:7). While caution is certainly a good idea, fear of making a commitment is a trap set for you which may keep you from knowing some good things God has intended for you. Fear is conquered through God's Word and prayer. I would encourage you to tackle that fear by pouring portions of Scripture into your head, reading and memorizing, and using it as the protection it is intended to be for us.

5

Common Mistakes in Relating to Our Friends

You could easily make a case that the relationship issues discussed in this chapter are not unique to singles, and with slight variations and some exceptions, I would agree. After all, relating to other people appropriately is basic in every arena with every type of person, and single people for the most part have the same problems as anyone else.

But I think there are some unique detours and twists for singles in relating to their friends which it may be helpful to discuss.

Mistake: We fail to allow for true friendships with the opposite sex, either for ourselves or for others.

When I was in college if you were seen alone with a person of the opposite sex, having a conversation that lasted more than five minutes, the rumors would start. Your roommate would collar you as soon as you were alone, having already heard through the grapevine about this encounter, and ask probing questions, such as, "Did he ask you out?" "Do you like him?" and so on.

It was virtually impossible to have a close friendship with someone of the opposite sex without being "tagged" as a couple, and once that word got out, no one else would come near. Now, that may be a slight exaggeration, but not much. That was twenty-five years ago, and I thought the new generation would have better sense. But my daughter discovered the same type atmosphere at her college, and I see it in singles groups in churches.

Once a group of us at college were discussing this unfortunate social dilemma, and we decided to try to change it. There were eight of us, four women and four men, and we secretly made a plan to date one another in rotation. We made a schedule so we would be seen with a different partner in fairly frequent succession, and all agreed not to tell anyone it was a plan. We were hoping to set a new trend on campus and convince people that it was much better to have freedom to be with many different people without having to worry about becoming a twosome.

It was great fun seeing my roommates and friends in the dorm totally confused and amazed to think I was dating Bob on Wednesday and Barry on Sunday. And then not long after that there were two other men and two different occasions. For a couple of weeks we had the campus buzzing. But it didn't take too long for someone to put two and two together and figure out what we were doing. Well, it was fun while it lasted, but we didn't change the unspoken social rule on the campus, which was, if you spent time with some man or woman, there had to be a romantic attraction.

There are difficulties in having close friendships with

the opposite sex, that's true. All too often one person sees it as a friendship while the other is secretly hoping it will grow into something else. But we need to allow for these friendships, for they are possible and they can be very wholesome. A friend was telling me just this past week that she has a male friend who is a business partner and who has befriended her for years. She would love to bring him to church, and feels certain he'd accept her invitation to join her each week. But she hesitates because if people see you sitting with the same man frequently, they inevitably assume it is a romantic involvement.

It becomes a dilemma. She wants him to be at church to hear God's Word clearly given each week. He doesn't get that input in his church. But if he came he would assume they would sit together—and why not; then she has to worry about what people think. That's rather sad, but I understood what she was telling me and her hesitancy to invite him.

Why can't we stop doing that to each other? Why can't we train ourselves not to automatically assume more than a friendship when we see two single people enjoying fellowship? I suppose the difficulty is that we can change our attitudes, but we can't make others change theirs and so we are forced to play by their rules.

I've had a friendship with a single man for over fifteen years, and he's been a wonderful gift to me. We made a decision early on that, for many good reasons, the relationship would never lead to marriage and it was truly a settled issue that this was a friendship and nothing more, in both our minds. But how nice it has been to have that male companionship, to get a male viewpoint, to be able to call him without worrying about what he might think, to go with him to concerts and weddings and parties. In other words, to have a friend in him just as I do with my female friends. However, I'll admit that many people still believed there was a romantic aspect to our relationship and no amount of denial convinced them otherwise. I think time has probably done that job for us.

The best we can do to remedy this situation is to keep ourselves from mentally linking people together without evidence, and keep reminding ourselves that a single man and woman truly can be just friends. And we can do what we can to help others change their mind-sets in this area.

Mistake: We tend to neglect our friendships when
we start to develop a dating relationship
with someone else.

As singles, our friendships have a special importance to us, don't you think? In many cases friends are truly our family, and because we don't have a marriage partner, we value those friendships perhaps even more than we would if married. So, when a close friend who's been in the same single-with-no-one-on-the-scene boat with us suddenly begins a new dating relationship, it can have a devastating effect on us.

First, we feel we're losing that close companionship because we no longer share the same predicament: no one to date. Second, we see their time now being occupied by that romantic interest, which obviously leaves less time for us. Third, it seems to drive home even more painfully the absence of a special relationship in our own life. We've lost our comrade-in-misery!

We need to work at this problem from both ends. The person who now has the other relationship certainly has obligations to the friendship which should not be ignored, and the person whose friend is now dating has some obligations as well.

All too often singles will neglect their friendships when they do become involved in a romantic relationship. Although that's not acceptable behavior in anyone's book, it's particularly painful to see Christians behave this way. Jesus told us that one of our distinguishing characteristics should be the love we have for each other. How can you love someone with God's kind of love, and then neglect him or her just because you've got another interest in your life?

To do that indicates an attitude toward friendships which is not admirable, and this is that friendships are valuable only as long as they are needed. Once something or someone comes along to better meet the need, the friendship loses importance.

Actually, a Christlike response would be to give even more careful attention to our friendships when we begin a dating relationship. If we recognize the difficulties that our friends may experience, our sensitivity should be greatly heightened to control that reaction as much as we can. You certainly don't have to feel guilty about your new relationship, but do be very sensitive. You may have been in that same position yourself. Remember how it felt. The Golden Rule sure works here (as it does everywhere): "Do unto others as you would have them do unto you."

Keep the same level of contact with your friends as you did before. Call them, make plans to be with them, take an interest in what's happening in their lives. Don't talk about your newfound friend all the time. Remember, their lives are still going on, and what happened to them this week is just as important as what happened with your new relationship.

Once a couple start to date, they seem to hold all their time for each other. So they are hesitant to make plans with their friends in case they might want to be with their boyfriend or girlfriend on that day. I was very pleased that my daughter still made plans with her friends just as she had before, after she started seriously dating Todd, who's now her husband. Her pattern of interacting with her friends didn't take a drastic turn just because the man of her dreams had come along.

You can also include your friends in your activities with your new friend, so that hopefully, you'll all be friends and the relationship expands rather than ends.

Let me add another word to my female readers here. Since usually the men ask us for dates, it is our lot to wait and see if they have plans for us to be together or not. This puts us in a rather delicate situation, especially when they tend to make plans at the last minute. But please don't allow that predicament to cause you to put your calendar on hold, hoping he will make plans.

I can remember doing that—just holding my breath each week until the weekend plans were set and refusing to make other plans until I knew for certain what his plans were for our weekend together. Big mistake! You should keep your social life going just as before and not hesitate to make plans or accept invitations from others that don't include him, even though you may have to turn down an invitation from him. Believe me, that could be the smartest thing you ever did. If you're always sitting there ready, never a conflict, never a problem, waiting for him to ask, you're sending him messages that aren't good, and you're neglecting other friendships.

On the other side of the coin, when a friend begins to date someone, we also have a responsibility to that friendship. We need to be careful that we don't make our friend feel guilty about the new relationship. And we certainly need to understand that it is going to take some time which might otherwise have been spent with us.

Again, my daughter's close friends were wonderful when she and Todd began to date. They were happy for her, and if they were envious, it didn't show. Their circle of friendship enlarged and they did many things together.

Friendships, especially among believers, are gifts from God. They need to be handled carefully and protected very well. You will need those friends whether they're going with someone or not. You'll want to be close even if they marry. There's no need for us to abandon or neglect our friendships just because we've found someone new and exciting.

Mistake: We tend to shun people who don't make us "look good."

Doesn't it seem that we gravitate toward people who fit our image and fulfill our expectations? We seem to seek friendships by what the other person will bring to our party. Will they make us look good? Will people think there's something wrong if we associate with that person?

This tendency may be a little more acute with us singles, since we're probably more image conscious when we're single. I think I've been very guilty of this at times. As I'm writing about it, I'm thinking of people I simply try to avoid if at all possible, because they aren't sharp or they have strange personalities. So, my own words convict me as I write them.

Obviously the basic problem here is selfishness, an attitude of "What can this person do for me?" Think of how Jesus associated with people who didn't make Him look good, and the religious leaders of His day loved to remind Him of this. On one occasion, they asked His disciples, "Why does your teacher eat with tax collectors and 'sinners'?" (Matthew 9:11). They had this same idea that you should shun people who don't make you look good.

Jesus was demonstrating a completely different viewpoint, one we need to incorporate into our thinking and actions toward people. As strange as it may seem, Jesus loves those people we find unlovely just as much as He loves us! And because of Jesus, it's possible for us to respond toward them in loving ways.

6

Common Mistakes in Relating to Married People

Have you noticed that singles and married couples don't tend to socialize with each other very often? Why is it we always head for people just like us? Well, obviously, it's because we have things in common, and to some degree that is understandable and reasonable.

However, I think Christians, of all people, should know unity, regardless of whether married or single. I struggle with the idea of singles ministries in churches, recognizing the need for this ministry, but at the same time wishing we could find a way to keep from separating singles and married people even more.

There is fault on both sides for this division. Both married people and singles perpetuate the problem with their attitudes and actions. I tackle the married people's attitude in chapter 11. Here I'll talk to us singles, with the hope that we can start to find ways to alleviate this unnecessary and nonproductive division in our Christian fellowships between married people and singles.

I'm so grateful that I have friends in both camps. My dearest and closest friend has been married forty years! I name many married couples among my close friendships, and of course, many singles as well. Their marital status is simply unimportant in their friendship with me.

I think many of us miss some wonderful relationships because of this "great divide." Having a variety of friends and relationships gives all of us a much better understanding of each other and a more realistic view of the world. We aren't as close-minded and we broaden our experience base nicely when we have a mixture of both single and married friends. What a shame that we've allowed this attitude to develop, especially among Christians.

I think we singles need to take a close look at our attitudes toward married people. Here are some common mistakes to consider.

Mistake: We put married people into a separate category and assume we have little or nothing in common.

Some dear friends, John and Afton, have been married almost two years now. They met in the singles class at their church and were very active in that class. They had many close friends within the group and other longtime friends who were single.

John and Afton have maintained those friendships since they were married. Their single friends are at their house frequently and they all still do things together. John's best friend is single, and he's as much a part of John's life as before. It's good to see that marriage hasn't diminished those friendships.

I remember John telling me right after they were married that their single friends showed some reluctance in coming over, as though they thought John and Afton wanted to be alone all the time! But with their gift of hospitality, they soon demonstrated that they wanted them to be as much a part of their lives as ever and that they needed their friendships.

As singles, we need to remind ourselves that married people need friendships, and if we've been friends in the past, they still need us. You don't enter some mystical world when you walk down the aisle. Having a marriage partner does not take the place of friendships. So, we need to find ways to maintain those friendships, even though there may be some changes in the relationship.

Obviously, it's a two-way street. Married couples have to show their desire and make an effort to keep the friendships alive, as John and Afton have done. There's no reason we have to lose those meaningful relationships in our lives because of marriage. (If you think I'm being hard on singles, jump ahead to chapter 11 and see what I have to say about the attitude of married people toward us singles!)

Mistake: Our feelings toward our married friends are affected by envy and jealousy.

A recently married couple told me that they had experienced "reverse discrimination" from their single friends. They were invited to a singles party, but upon arriving, the first words they heard were, "Oh, here's those married people." Throughout the evening, they felt ostracized, as though their presence was resented, since they were now married.

Could it be that we Christian singles ventilate our frustrations at still being single by treating our now-married formerly single friends as if they no longer have anything in common with us? Could we be guilty of spiteful behavior toward them because they got married and we didn't?

That should never happen in the Body of Christ. The Apostle John said that the world will know we are disciples of Christ by the love we have for each other. Obviously, a reverse discrimination toward married friends is not an attitude of love.

Many singles have expressed to me their strong dislike for weddings. Sitting through someone else's wedding, especially that of a close friend, is indeed a sharp reminder that we're still single.

Weddings can have that effect on us, and I understand the reaction. But as Christians we have to go back to God's sovereignty and ask ourselves if we really believe God has a purpose and is in control of our lives. If we do, then as we discussed in chapter 1, we must come to terms with our singleness, not just accepting it, but believing that God has good and wonderful purposes for us while single.

When we're envious of someone else, we're really saying, "God, I could have done a better job of ordering my life than You. Someone else has it better than me, so You're not fair, God, and You're not doing what's best for me." Envy and jealousy are indications of a lack of trust on our part. They are also sinful. Scripture is very strong on these two points.

> But if you harbor bitter envy and selfish ambition in your hearts, do not boast about it or deny the truth. Such "wisdom" does not come down from heaven but is earthly, unspiritual, of the devil. For where you have envy and selfish ambition, there you find disorder and every evil practice.
>
> James 3:14–16

James certainly didn't have any difficulty expressing his feelings, did he? Those are strong words. Selfish ambition is wanting something for yourself that satisfies your own needs, and envy is wanting what someone else has to satisfy your own needs. Very similar. These two things lead to disorder and sinful practices.

Is it possible that we singles can be so possessed by our desire to be married that it turns into envy and selfish ambition? Obviously, the answer is yes. Sometimes we take those feelings out on our married friends and either drop the friendship or treat it poorly.

Peter tells us in 1 Peter 2:1 that we must rid ourselves of all envy. How do we rid ourselves of the envy and jealousy we feel toward married people? Well, that takes us back to chapter 1 again, for we must resolve our attitude toward marriage before we'll be able to stop envying married people. It begins in our thought life, as we refuse to allow ourselves to think enviously of those who are married.

You know, when you start digging underneath your attitudes, you're likely to find all kinds of sinful residue that you didn't know was there. Underneath that disdain for weddings may be ugly envy, which is leading to disorder and sin in your life. Hidden behind your reluctance to be with your married friends may be the sinful dregs of jealousy because they're married and you're not. It could be the root cause of other problems in your life. James says it leads to disorder and every evil practice.

Mistake: We sometimes allow a relationship with a married person to develop beyond acceptable boundaries.

I've talked about maintaining friendships with married people, and I certainly think that's important. But I cannot ignore a problem that occurs all too often, when a single person develops a relationship with someone of the opposite sex who's married, and it goes beyond acceptable boundaries.

As singles we work with married people and associate with them in many different environments. Usually in these situations we get to know only one half of that married couple, because the other person is not around. So it's easy to forget that the person is married.

Here are some strong suggestions and guidelines for these relationships with married people. First, ask about their family frequently. Show strong interest in their children, what they're doing, what their wife or husband does, and so on.

At one point in my career, I had a manager who was giving signals of being attracted to me. I would make it a point to ask about his family, particularly his wife, every chance I could, especially when we were by ourselves. I also looked for opportunities to compliment and admire his wife and children. That certainly sends a strong signal to anyone who has wrong ideas about your relationship.

Second, don't ever get caught up in listening to and commiserating with him or her about home situations. It doesn't matter how sad the story may be or how much your friend may need a listening ear, if you're single and of the opposite sex, you're *not* the right person to give comfort or counsel. Personally, I would not allow any exceptions to this guideline, even if you have no suspicions about their motives in talking with you. I've seen too many affairs begin with those "innocent" talks, when someone was just trying to be a friend.

If you work closely with a married person, and you get along well, plan an occasion to meet his or her mate in a social setting and get to know the other half of that couple. I have several male friends who were my peers in business, and their wives and I are now good friends. We get together socially and stay in touch, but the relationship I have is with the families, not just with the men. When we were working together, I was conscious of not doing or saying anything that would ever give their wives any reason to wonder for a minute about my relationship with their husbands.

If you sense you are becoming attracted to a married person, take drastic action fast! Sometimes I think we can find married people more attractive than single people.

There is something about forbidden fruit that appeals to our sinful, fleshly nature. We need to recognize that tendency and be prepared to run fast away from it. The Apostle Paul told us to flee sexual immorality (1 Corinthians 6:18). My dear friends, please hear me clearly on this point. You cannot afford to give your sexual desires an inch. They move in on you so fast, you'll never know what hit you. Do yourself a favor and run as fast as you can away from any attraction you begin to feel for someone who is married. Don't stop to rationalize; don't ask anyone's opinion; don't give it weeks and months of consideration. Move and move fast.

That may mean changing jobs or changing churches. It may mean asking for a transfer. It may mean going out of your way to avoid contact with that person. But whatever you think you have to do, do more. So many times we say, "Oh, I can handle it." That's our first mistake. First Corinthians 10:12 warns us, "So, if you think you are standing firm, be careful that you don't fall!" If there's ever a time not to trust yourself, it's when sexual or physical attraction is involved.

Familiarity and casualness about sex-related topics is very common today. People think nothing of talking about sexual matters in almost any setting. Don't get squeezed into the world's mold and allow yourself to be caught in these kinds of conversations. Have the courage to walk away from the conversation, even if your actions are obvious. Although we need to act with as much kindness as possible, we shouldn't feel awkward about letting people know we don't approve of certain topics of conversation.

We've all seen how the testimony of evangelical Christians has been damaged by people who thought they could handle a situation and then ended up in sexual sins that were headlined across every newspaper in America. I guarantee you they never thought it would go that far. But they allowed the door to open just that first little bit, and it was downhill from there.

If we would just realize that we cannot give the flesh one small opportunity, we could save ourselves so much grief and prevent these sinful relationships from ever beginning.

Though it's happened to me quite a few times, I'm still amazed to discover that when people write or call to talk with me about their affairs, they are usually rationalizing and justifying their behavior because of their circumstances and looking to me for support in their predicament. "I'm married but I haven't lived with my husband for two years." "He's married, but he doesn't sleep with his wife." "He's married and his wife won't give him a divorce." "But we really love each other."

As I listen to these stories, what I hear is despair, pain, hopelessness. These affairs they are trying to justify and feel they cannot live without have made their lives miserable, and usually they've affected a few other lives as well. Several have even talked about killing themselves, but not about breaking the relationship.

When I give them biblical counsel to immediately cut that relationship and ask God's forgiveness, my heart sinks in most cases because I hear or see a reaction that says, "I can't do that." So, they continue to pay the price for sexual immorality, and that price is extremely high.

If these people had run the other way the first time they

felt an attraction for that married person, how much pain and sorrow they could have avoided, how the name of Christ could have been honored instead of dragged through the mud, and how many other people would have been spared the disgrace and disruption caused by those affairs.

Well, there's no question that both sides need to rethink their attitudes, both singles and married people. There's no reason we have to be separated from each other and not enjoy the friendships and encouragement that each can give the other. Perhaps some of these thoughts may be helpful to you in establishing better relationships with your married friends.

7

Common Mistakes in Relating to Family Members

Families, like people, are totally unique. No two are alike. The way my family interacts and relates will be different from yours, so there is no one role model or ideal that has to be followed by everyone. Certainly, learning to relate well to our families is not a singles issue as such. It's a relational issue that everyone faces.

We need our families. God gave us this basic unit as the foundation for society. Even though the family has been degraded or neglected by much of our humanistic thinking, nothing can change the fact that we need our families. We're built that way by God.

So, let's consider some roadblocks we singles face in trying to establish and maintain close relationships with our family members.

Mistake: We allow the inappropriate attitudes of family members toward our singleness to inhibit our relationship with them.

While it's true that single adults now number over 37 percent of the adult population in America, if you're the single adult in your family, among mostly married people, frequently you can feel like the two-headed monster. Sometimes the very atmosphere in family gatherings reeks with the question: "Why aren't you married like the rest of us? What's the matter with you?"

So many times the first question we hear from our family is "Who are you going with now?" or "Any romantic interest in your life?" or "Okay, tell us what's happening with you," which translated mean "Do you have any marriage plans in the future?"

In chapter 11, I address the attitude of others toward singles, and I just hope that somehow the people who should read that chapter will read it. But now I'm talking about how we react to these attitudes. Take it from me, no matter how many books they read, some of your family members will never change their attitude toward singleness, and you're always going to be faced with handling their remarks and attitudes as long as you're single.

So, what do we do? Have a lecture ready every time they say something? Stay away from those family members who bug us too much about being single? Grin and bear it?

Well, the thing we don't want is for their attitudes to drive us away from our family and good relations with family members. We need our families, there's no two ways about it. I come from a close family group, with two brothers who are married, eight nieces and nephews, and a growing number of great grandchildren now entering the scene. We don't live near one another, but we stay close. I can't imagine not staying in touch with my family or not knowing what's happening in their lives.

After I was divorced, I could have withdrawn from my family. After all, family occasions were somewhat uncomfortable those first few years, no one was exactly sure what to say or not say, and it wasn't quite the same. But had I withdrawn I would have lost so much. It might have saved me some embarrassment and discomfort at first, but those family ties and support are extremely vital to me, as they are to all of us.

Don't allow anything to disturb whatever closeness you have with your family. Overlook attitudes that bother you or, if appropriate, find a way to discuss your feelings with your family. At the same time, find ways to bond yourself even closer to your family.

Are you careful to give your family the attention they deserve? Or is your life too busy and hectic to do those little things you should? How about birthday cards and phone calls? Many times singles neglect these family occasions, as though they don't have to send cards or gifts until they're married.

Find a way to remind yourself of every one of your family members' birthdays, and at least get a card off to them. I keep everyone's birthdays listed on my calendar, otherwise, I'd never remember. But it's easy enough to do with a simple reminder, and the family really appreciates it. Even if they don't all send you cards, you do it for them. It will help strengthen those ties if you make the first move and reach out.

Remember, your family members are people, too, with needs and hurts. They may think *you* don't care. Married people generally tend to think that we singles are all too occupied with our own lives to truly care about theirs. We need to dispel that feeling. Just call and talk to those brothers or sisters or cousins you haven't seen in a while. Listen to what's going on in their lives. Show that you consider them important.

Mistake: We allow past hurts to ruin present family relationships.

It's likely that many of you reading this book are dealing with hurts from your past brought on by family members. I realize how difficult that can be to deal with, especially if there was abusive treatment of any kind. In some cases reconciliation may not be possible, but many times we keep ourselves apart from our families unnecessarily.

I have a friend who has not talked with her mother for many months. I know that her mother can be tedious to deal with, but I wonder if that's sufficient justification for cutting off communications with your mother. Your parents may not have been the best in the world and they may have failed to give you the childhood you needed in some aspects. But in most cases their failures were the result of failed role models and examples in their own lives, and rarely were intentional.

Besides, the biblical teaching on forgiveness is pretty clear. We are to forgive those who've wronged us, regardless. Until we do, we'll find no healing for the pains of those relationships.

The humanistic thinking and psychological philosophies of the past several decades have led people to blame their parents and family situation for every problem they face. Counselors have frequently advised people to break relationships with family members in order to "find themselves" and "be their own person." The exaggerated focus on individual rights and freedoms has led us to mistreat close family ties, and that is very destructive because God has made us to be a part of a family, and nothing can replace our family relationships.

Even if your family relationships are not everything you want them to be, don't neglect them. Remember that God has said He will receive us even when our mother or father forsake us (Psalm 27:10) and trust that the Lord can fill in the missing pieces we experience because of past or present family problems. But meanwhile, do all you can to keep some kind of relationship going with your family, even if it's not all you want it to be.

In relating to our family members, we simply need to make certain that being single does not mean we're too busy to stay in close touch or that we stay away because we're uncomfortable as a single among married family members. Nor should we let past failures on anyone's part keep us from trying again to establish a loving relationship with our family. We need them; they need us.

8

Common Mistakes in Financial and Career Matters

I often think how nice it would be if money never had to be a consideration! It just seems to muddy up the waters very frequently, doesn't it? But it's a fact of life, and a very real one.

Of course, career decisions have a lot to do with financial matters, not to mention job satisfaction, challenging work, and so on. So, it makes sense for us to think about how we handle financial matters as well as career decisions and circumstances.

Here are some areas concerning financial matters and careers which we singles need to consider closely.

Mistake: Our financial planning is usually weak or nonexistent.

Savings accounts, retirement planning, insurance, IRA's, investments, real estate—those are for married people, right? Unfortunately, many single people seem to have that idea. Since most of us—especially in our twenties—

keep assuming we'll be married one of these days, we simply postpone these matters until then.

Well, that's a mistake. As soon as you have a regular income, you need to do some financial planning. Even if you think you don't have enough income to worry about, you really do need a plan that will establish good stewardship of your money.

My niece married in her late twenties, so she and her husband spent several years as singles in good careers. They both were careful about finances from the beginning of their careers, so that when they married, they had something to show for their single years and they brought good financial habits into the marriage.

Susan had bought a house on her own, and so had Danny. They were able to sell one when they married, which gave them some needed cash. Also, before they were married, they decided to attend Larry Burkett's seminar for Christians on financial planning and budgeting. This has given them a very solid biblical perspective of the use of their money, and from the beginning of their marriage, they've practiced what they learned at the seminar.

As singles they were certainly able to spend more money on themselves than they are now, with two children. Budgeting, too, was not as essential when single as they feel it is now, with two people involved in the financial decisions.

Both agree that singles can become really good stewards of their financial resources by learning and practicing good budgetary habits. For one thing, putting some money away each month for "impulse" spending, gives you that little cash reserve which allows you to take advantage of sudden opportunities—like a spur-of-the-moment weekend trip—without feeling guilty or worrying about the impact on your finances.

Perhaps this is an area where you've been irresponsible in the past. For some reason many of us feel that we don't have to be as responsible with our money when we're single as we plan to be when we're married. But that simply is erroneous thinking. With more and more people marrying later in life, we frequently have several years of income before marrying, and that income should be carefully managed. You'll be glad you did, whether you marry or not.

Mistake: We tend to be less faithful in giving money to the Lord's work.

I wonder if Christian singles give proportionately as much of their income to the Lord as married people do. Certainly some singles do; some give more. But with less accountability as to how our money is used, we may find it easier to compromise our commitment to give back to the Lord a good portion of what He has given us.

I think the unfortunate second-class-citizen attitude toward singles that we frequently find in churches (addressed in chapter 11) may at times cause singles to feel less obligated or committed to their church's financial needs. After all, we may think, if the married people are going to run the church and hold the major places of leadership and importance, they can provide the money as well.

But, just as we discussed in the chapter on dealing with our families, we don't want to let other people's wrong attitudes cause us to have wrong attitudes or rob us of the joy of supporting God's work financially. Have you experienced the incredible joy of giving to the Lord, even giving what you think you don't have to give? I am a beginner in that school, but I can tell you from my small experience and the larger experience of many Christians I know that it opens up an avenue of service to God which is thrilling. When God gives us earthly money, He's looking to see how well we use it for eternal, heavenly purposes. When we use our money for His glory, we are storing up treasures in heaven.

All my life I've heard the verse about storing up treasures in heaven, and where your treasure is there your heart will be too. But it's only in the last few years that it has started to really dawn on me how wonderful it is to know that I've spent money here on earth that has gone directly to heaven, and it's on the books there.

Certainly money is not the only investment we can send ahead of us to heaven. Time is another, and in my opinion, it's often more difficult for us to part with than our money. But discover the excitement of spending money here on earth which is going ahead of you to heaven. That is such a marvelous privilege. When this very short earthly life is ended, we'll stand there in heaven with some treasures sent on ahead of us. Now, that really is exciting. How wonderful if more of us could know the joy of giving instead of viewing it as a duty or responsibility.

Mistake: We spend too much money on "good times" and indulge our impulses too much.

This certainly is a broad general statement, because some singles are very frugal and careful with their money. But I have noticed in myself and others a tendency to spend money more impulsively. Someone says, "Hey, let's go out to dinner tonight," and even though our budget says no, our desire to be with others and not eat alone causes us to say yes. We spend the fifteen or twenty dollars for dinner, enjoy the time with our friends, but later when we're by ourselves, we think, *Oh, great, that was my pocket change for the rest of the week. Now, what am I going to do?* It seems difficult to get together for any social occasion without dropping some money, and that ten dollars here and there really add up fast.

There are some underlying causes of this carelessness with our funds. Many times we spend the money we shouldn't spend because we're embarrassed to say, "You know, I just can't afford it right now." It's often because we really want to be with our friends, and that need outweighs our need to be frugal. We sacrifice the future for the present. Also, we aren't accountable to anyone for how we spend our money, so we lack the control that comes from accountability.

While we may not have earthly accountability, we

certainly need to remember that we will give account to the Lord of how we've used our resources. If you feel this is a problem in the management of your finances, I have a few suggestions.

Prepare yourself mentally to resist impulse spending. Pray about it, and ask the Lord to give you strength to resist it. On days when you know the opportunity will be likely to arise, for instance on Sundays at church or certain evenings after work, talk to yourself about what your limits are. Make a commitment to yourself and to the Lord that you will not spend beyond a certain amount, whatever your budget allows. Be prepared mentally for those impulsive spending situations.

Also, don't window-shop too often. I've noticed that if I don't go looking at what there is to buy, I don't even perceive I have a need. But let me start shopping a bit, and the bargains look too good to pass up. When you do shop, have a definite purpose in mind, find what you need, and avoid the tendency to look at everything else. If you're like most of us, the window-shopping just feeds your appetite and convinces you that you need what you really don't need.

Also, don't be hesitant or embarrassed to make alternative suggestions in order to save money. For instance, you could suggest a restaurant that is less expensive or you could open your home and invite people to join you there for pizza or peanut butter and jelly sandwiches! I can assure you many others will appreciate your efforts to hold down the spending; they've probably wanted to do it but didn't have the nerve!

Another good idea might be to establish some earthly

accountability. Make yourself accountable to someone you trust; ask that person to help you; report regularly, and use that accountability to establish the frugal habits that you need.

Mistake: We often make career decisions with very short-term vision.

Though this is definitely changing as we see people marrying later in life, singles often have a tendency not to get serious about a career until we have responsibilities, like marriage and children. Singles have tended to flounder in a career, make more changes, and be less concerned about job opportunities. In a sense, being single is helpful in young careers, because it gives you more flexibility to make changes as you are discovering what kind of a job really appeals to you. But we shouldn't allow that flexibility to make us appear uncommitted or frivolous about career decisions.

One thing prospective employers look at closely when considering a new employee is his or her tenure at other jobs. If you show a pattern of changing jobs every year or so, that sends up a danger signal to someone who's reading your résumé. I've been in the position of reading résumés and searching for new employees, and one of the first things I look at is tenure in past jobs.

Just recently one of my clients said to me, "I'm not hiring anyone else in their twenties. They have no intention of making a career commitment, and you know they'll be gone just about the time you get them trained." I think we've developed a climate in our business society where the employee feels little or no loyalty to the employer. That generates a lower level of job performance, which in turn generates a lower level of loyalty from the employer to the employee. It becomes a cycle, and you wonder which came first, the chicken or the egg, lack of employee loyalty or lack of employer loyalty?

Certainly this inclination is not limited to single people, but we are more susceptible to it than married people because of our freedom to move around more easily. You would be well advised to think much more carefully about the jobs you take and go into them with a mind-set that says, "I'm going to give it all I've got and do everything possible to make this job a good one." If you take a job with the attitude that you're just going to get some experience so you can get a better job, it's unfair to your employer and will be adversely reflected in your performance. Certainly that doesn't mean you have to make a lifetime commitment to a job, but your attitude toward your employer should be one of service, not one of using the employer to achieve your own goals.

In this age where it's every man for himself and where greed has become an accepted way of life for many, we, as Christians, must constantly beware of allowing ourselves to be shoved into that mold. Ephesians 6:7 says we are to serve our masters wholeheartedly, as if we "were serving the Lord, not men, because you know that the Lord will reward everyone for whatever good he does. . . ."

Remember, you will give an account to God for the quality of your work for your employer. Just stop and imagine yourself, right now, standing before God, explaining the performance you've been giving to your employer. Would you be ashamed to do that today? Would you be confronted with a lazy attitude toward your employer, designed to take advantage of what the job offers you without giving back good service in return?

Mistake: Women too often make career decisions with "Mr. Right" in mind.

Even with twenty-five years of "women's liberation" behind us, many single women still approach life with only one goal or desire: to be married. They find it difficult to imagine that they will ever have to take their jobs seriously, because, after all, Mr. Right will be along someday soon to rescue them from the working world.

Now, I know that has changed for many women, but believe me, I also know it still lingers in the minds of lots of us single women. Even in the midst of my career climb, when I was "blazing new paths" for women in sales and making a name for myself in the business world, in the back of my mind was that ever-present mind-set that it was temporary. Prince Charming would be along any day to offer me the financial security that would eliminate this need to worry about jobs or money.

I well remember the first time I had the thought that I might really have to take care of myself financially for the rest of my life. Maybe I'm a slow learner, but it was at least six or seven years into my career before I gave that possibility any serious consideration—and the thought shocked me. I didn't like it; I didn't want to think about it.

This goes back to our discussion in chapters 1 and 2 about our attitudes toward marriage. A wrong perspective of marriage affects many other areas, and it surely will affect our career choices and job performance.

Mistake: Women have a fear of being too successful in a career.

I remember a business associate from years back, a single woman who had quickly been promoted into a high-level management job, which was a much better job than most of her single male peers had. She was not a believer, but she was very concerned that her job status would inhibit her social life and her ability to attract men. She once told me, "When I meet a man, I don't tell him what my job is. I avoid it as long as possible. As soon as they hear I'm a branch manager for such a big company, it frightens them off."

Her statement amazed me. I was just getting started in my career with IBM, and that problem had never occurred to me. But since then I've experienced it myself and know many other women who share the same feeling. A woman who displays the abilities, leadership, and intelligence required for advancement in business becomes a threat to many men. The more successful we are, the more we narrow our field of eligible men.

I've become resigned to this phenomenon, but I can easily understand the frustrations younger women feel as they are faced with these alternatives. It's very frustrating to realize that men can pursue success to any extent they choose without jeopardizing any potential relationships. If a man makes far more money than a woman to whom he's attracted, all the better. If his job title is more impressive than a woman's, that's an asset for him. But not so with single women.

As a result many single women purposely limit their career pursuits to avoid placing themselves in positions that are better than those of their average male peers. Or they take the promotions and positions offered, fearing the consequences to their potential for marriage.

I honestly don't know any way we'll change this attitude in our society, and my only advice is that you make your decisions carefully and prayerfully. It personally bothers me to see a woman limit herself because of this attitude, since I feel God expects us to do all we can with the resources and talents He has given us. I've often thought and said that God is not inefficient. He would never give me or any woman abilities and potential and then not allow us to use them to their fullest.

Now, this whole question has to be considered in the light of God's will for our individual lives, and I'm well aware that it's quite possible to use the abilities God has given us in ways that He did not intend for us to use them. But assuming that you, as a woman, are in the position you feel God has for you at this point in your life, I would encourage you to pursue your work with everything you have, and let God take care of the consequences. He is still God and He is still sovereign. We can trust Him with our success, just as we can trust Him when we fail.

We also need to be careful to be modest about our accomplishments, in order not to unnecessarily drive a wedge between ourselves and our male peers. But we don't have to be ashamed of them. After all, whatever we have done is simply by God's grace and because of His gifts to us. We should be truly humble that God has been good to us, but never ashamed to tell of His goodness.

How difficult it is in this generation to avoid judging people by salaries, titles, experience, possessions, and the like. The more we can change our own thinking to realize that God does not measure success in these terms, the less difficulty we'll have with this issue.

9

Common Mistakes in Our Life-styles

There are many advantages to the single life-style, and I think they outweigh the disadvantages. The freedom we have to set our own pace, make our own decisions, change our plans, spend our money, and prioritize our time—to mention a few—are wonderful gifts and resources. Until you've relinquished those freedoms, you don't really appreciate how nice they are!

Whenever I start to feel sorry for myself because of some aspect of my single life-style—like no one to help me lug the bags of salt for the water softener to the basement or no one to go to dinner with me on a moment's notice—I simply remind myself of how wonderful it is not to have to report to anyone concerning how I spend my discretionary time or money. How nice it is not to have to feel guilty if my schedule doesn't fit in with someone else's. How much time I save because I don't have the responsibilities of having to cook meals on a regular basis, and on and on.

I'm quite certain my married friends, though they might not admit it, would love to have some of these luxuries of the single life-style again. One tendency we all have is to think that the grass on the other side is greener, and it's very helpful for us singles to simply count the blessings of the single life-style and enjoy them while we have them. So often singles miss out on the enjoyment of being single because they're busy peering over the fence and longing for the grass of the married life.

However, even with all the good aspects of the single life-style, there are some easy traps into which we can fall if we're not careful. Let me mention four that are fairly common.

Mistake: We want to keep our options open, which can lead to irresponsibleness.

One reputation singles have in Christian communities and social settings is that it's difficult to get them to make a commitment and keep it. While this is very much a "bum rap" for many singles who are extremely dependable, it is true in all too many instances.

There is undoubtedly more than one contributing factor to this reputation, but I believe the major one is the mind-set of many singles that they have to keep their options open for the best offer. After all, if I agree to help at a church dinner on Saturday evening, two weeks in advance, I may in the meantime have to turn down a date or a social invitation that I want to accept. Who knows what could come up in two weeks?

Let's face it, when you are single, especially if you live alone or have no other people for whom you are respon- sible, such as children, it's not difficult to become self-focused. Who else do you really have to consider but yourself? If a single person is not involved in reaching out to other people, that lack of accountability or responsibility to others can produce a selfish life-style.

We are born self-centered; it is a characteristic of our sinful nature, and even when we're born anew from above, that sinful self keeps crawling up on the throne of our hearts always trying to be number one. It's a battle we all face throughout our lives, until we are with Christ and have a new body and a completely new nature. Until then, taking self off the throne and putting Christ and others there is a lifelong, daily task.

More and more I'm realizing the radicalness of our call by Christ to be servants. Who of us would ever aspire to servanthood? When you were asked as a kid what you wanted to be when you grew up, did you ever say, "I want to be a servant"? No way. Serving goes against our natures, but Jesus made it abundantly clear that it is a requirement for discipleship.

Christian singles are not excepted. We have the same call, and with the freedom we have with our time and resources, we need to remember that to whom much is given, much is required.

Have you been reluctant to take responsibilities or make commitments to people in order to keep your options open? That is certainly not a servant life-style.

Have you developed a reputation of being undependable? This can be a result of this "open-option" thinking, too. Singles can bail out on commitments pretty quickly if something more attractive comes on the scene.

Several years ago I headed the singles ministry at our

church for a few months, while we were in the process of searching for a new minister of singles. We tackled some projects that were ambitious, and most of the singles were terrific at pitching in and making things happen. But I well remember getting messages from singles at the last minute that "they couldn't make it," and having no-shows who had promised to help in the kitchen, with no explanation whatsoever. Of course, I realize that singles are not the only ones who can be irresponsible, but I do think many singles develop a mind-set that causes them to be careless with their commitments.

Let me hasten to say here, as I think about our own church, that if it weren't for some singles there, many jobs would go undone. There are most definitely two sides to this coin, so if this shoe doesn't fit you, just throw it out!

Mistake: We become set in our ways.

I really am tempted not to include this one, because it hits a little too close to home for me! I realize that after many years of living by myself, especially the last six with my daughter away at college and now married, I've developed my own comfortable way of doing things and I don't like to have it disturbed.

While routines can be good and helpful things, especially in the self-discipline area, they can also be controlling. We may discover that we are controlled by our way of doing things, and it can become an obsession.

The stereotype of the bachelor or "old maid" who does

everything the same way all the time and won't ever change the routine may be somewhat exaggerated, but we need to be aware of these tendencies. Living with someone else—whether mate, child, or roommate—helps keep us flexible, and if we don't have that environment, then we have to work at it.

I try to make myself change my routines from time to time, just to discipline myself against this inflexible attitude. One of my constant prayers is that God will keep me teachable, able to change and grow, and not set in my ways!

When you analyze it, an inflexible life-style with routines that cannot be disturbed and schedules that are sacred is again part of that self-focused attitude. It's saying, "I want to do it my way and no other way." It's a subtle declaration that *my* plans, *my* "order of service," *my* procedures are of highest importance and obviously are best.

Oh, how subtle that pride monster is. You pick up almost any rock, and there is lurks underneath. Even in something as seemingly innocent as a rigid life-style, we can discover that the rigidity is in large part pride.

Of course, it can also be a comfort zone. We do things the way we always have because it's familiar territory, we don't have to think about it, we don't have to take any risks, there's much less chance of failure. Surely laziness or fear of the unknown can be significant contributing factors to our status-quo mentality.

Well, this is getting a little too close to home, so enough said!

Mistake: We can easily become workaholics.

For various reasons, it's fairly easy for a single career person to put all his or her time and effort into that career, and work night and day. Obviously for some it is simply ambition, the desire to get ahead fast. For others, it's time on their hands, nobody to go home to, nothing to do tonight, so work becomes the choice.

There's nothing wrong with working hard and long. Certainly while you're single you can do that with less negative impact than after you're married. I suppose if the hours I work were ever added up, some people would describe me as a workaholic. I can be that way if I'm not careful.

The fine line we walk here is motive and balance. Why do you work long and hard? Are you obsessed with ambition and drive? That certainly is not a biblical attitude. Do you work to keep from facing other realities, like an empty house or apartment? Running from reality is like putting a Band-Aid on cancer, it doesn't solve anything.

If you find that you're becoming a workaholic, losing yourself in your work for whatever reason, one suggestion is to get involved in someone else's life. Many churches or social agencies have pal programs, where adults take a child as a pal, usually a child from a single-parent home or an underprivileged home. What an incredible difference you could make in a child's life simply by spending a night each week with him or her, showing love and attention.

There are Crisis Pregnancy Centers that need counselors, youth programs at church that need leaders—many ways to become involved in the life of someone who really needs your touch or help. When you start to do something like that, the focus shifts from yourself to someone else, and it's amazing how your perspective about your own life-style changes.

Mistake: Lack of accountability allows us to live a "double life."

Without personal accountability in our lives, we are extremely vulnerable to life-style slippage, falling into patterns of living that do not honor Christ and getting by with it because no one knows or has a right to say anything if they do.

How many Christian singles can be found in singles bars? How many live immorally, having affairs and romantic involvements that go far beyond biblical limits? How many are into pornography? How many Christian singles watch R-rated and X-rated movies, especially now when they can be rented and viewed in our own homes? Of course, these things are not limited to Christian *singles*, but our lack of accountability gives us more opportunity to fall into these traps.

From my mail and my knowledge of Christian singles, as well as my own ten-year sabbatical from my commitment to Jesus Christ, I know that life-style slippage is very common. We can show up at church on Sundays, saying all the right things and making all the right moves, but if our life-style were exposed for what it is, many times it would reveal a double life.

This should not be tagged as a mistake, but rather as a

sin. There's no other word to describe this double life-style. Frequently it has its beginnings in self-pity. I know singles who feel sorry for themselves because they can't find anyone special at church, after trying for years, so they go back to their old ways, or perhaps they start some new ways, hitting the singles bars and so on—"Looking for love in all the wrong places," as the song puts it.

It doesn't take great insight to recognize that this life-style slippage problem begins when our own per-ceived needs take priority over our commitment to Jesus Christ. In fact, my experience is that the slippage in the integrity of our life-styles is in direct proportion to the importance of the Word of God in our lives and the time we spend in prayer. As those things take less and less priority, the life-style slippage becomes more and more severe.

Many singles have the attitude that God owes them a Christian partner. When God doesn't deliver within cer-tain acceptable time frames, He gets blamed, and these singles walk away from their commitment to Christ.

Our humanistic philosophies have shaped our thinking in such distorted ways that we see God as a useful servant in our quest for whatever it is we think will make us happy. And for the single person, marriage is usually where we think it's at! Happiness is the central focus, and God is a handy method we can use to help us find it.

Our understanding of God is warped beyond belief, and that always gets us into trouble. The more we know who God is—not who we think He is or who we want Him to be, but who He *is* as defined in the Bible—the less we'll see Him as our "Santa Claus in the Sky." We were created for God's purposes, not the other way around, and He alone is sovereign.

We come to God on His terms if we come at all. And while it's abundantly true that He desires to do good things for us and has good plans for us, it is also abundantly true that we don't dictate the terms. Coming to God on His terms immediately changes our mind-set that God owes us anything. He is not in our debt. He has a right to do whatever He pleases with lives that He has created and redeemed. We are not our own; we've been bought for a price. When that is clear in our thinking, everything else starts to take its proper place. Life-style slippage has to go. The double life cannot exist when God is the focus of our thinking and our greatest desire is to please Him.

Well, we have to fight this tendency of allowing our life-styles to fall into sinful patterns. The most important and absolutely essential antidote for life-style slippage is God's Word and prayer. If you don't regularly have time with God, significant time—not four minutes snatched while you're eating breakfast—you can count on life-style slippage occurring. That has to be our highest priority.

Another key element in fighting back is to develop some accountability for ourselves. Since it doesn't come naturally through a marriage partner, perhaps we have to put our own accountability structures in place. That's where a pastor, a good friend, a small group, or a family member can be so valuable to us.

When I lived in Chicago, I had a weekly Bible study group for five years or so, and the accountability of that group was marvelous. With love and great caring, we kept track of one another. Each week as we met, after Bible study, we shared what had happened in the past week, and many times we shared failures. There were those in the group struggling with life-style problems, relationships that should not be, and so on, and the group accountability, love, and support gave them the strength they needed to change. In great love we confronted each other when necessary. But this kind of trust and openness came through time together, a shared priority that Jesus Christ should be first in our lives, and a willingness to be vulnerable. We need more of these small groups, which get together for accountability and support purposes, not strictly social reasons.

10

Common Mistakes in Our Commitment to Jesus Christ

This book is written to Christian singles; therefore, I make an assumption as I write that the reader is indeed a Christian. However, since I have no control over who reads this book, it seems appropriate that the label of Christian should be clearly defined, to make certain we're talking the same language.

Since I believe the Bible to be the infallible Word of God as given originally and inerrant in its truth and the only source of truth, I will simply share the Bible's definition of what it is to be a Christian. You will hear other definitions from other people, but if they differ, they are not Bible definitions, they are simply opinions.

Since I wouldn't trust my own opinion in such a critical area, I surely wouldn't expect anyone else to either. So, this is not my opinion or my interpretation; it is clear biblical teaching, over which there simply can be no serious controversy. Some things in Scripture are not so clear, but the definition of a Christian is abundantly explicit.

Jesus said to Nicodemus that "God so loved the world

that he gave his one and only Son, that whoever believes in him shall not perish but have eternal life" (John 3:16). He also told us that He is the way, the truth, and the life, and no one comes to the Father (God) except through Him, Jesus Christ (John 14:6). In Romans 10:9 we read that "if you confess with your mouth, 'Jesus is Lord,' and believe in your heart that God raised him from the dead, you will be saved." Paul pointed out that His message was one of repentance and faith: "I have declared to both Jews and Greeks that they must turn to God in repentance and have faith in our Lord Jesus" (Acts 20:21).

According to biblical teaching, a Christian is a person who has at some point in his life recognized his sin problem, realized that he was a sinner by nature and by willful habit, and at the same time, admitted that he is helpless to change that sinful nature. That person who then believes that Jesus is the true Son of God, and that by His death on Calvary He paid the penalty for our sins, and who then accepts Christ's redemptive death as payment for his or her own personal sin, has by that belief become a child of God. All people are God's creation, but it's only by coming to God through Jesus Christ that we become His child.

Believing in Christ is more than a mental assent to the historical reality of Jesus. It is an acceptance of Him as the Redeemer and Lord of your life. It includes a purposeful turning from the sins of your past. You could not be a Christian, born from above, and not know it. It doesn't sneak up on you. It isn't inherited from your parents or grandparents. It has nothing to do with how good a person you are, for you can never earn the redemption Christ offers you. It is a free gift.

Once you become a Christian, it makes a difference in you. Paul says, "Therefore, if anyone is in Christ, he is a new creation; the old has gone, the new has come!" (2 Corinthians 5:17).

Do you know for certain that you have become a Christian? Have you just assumed you were since you've gone to church all your life?

Well, if there's any question in your mind, I would strongly urge you to stop right now and get that issue settled. You'll probably need more insight into Scripture than the brief explanation I've given here. Find someone who can help, or go to your local Christian bookstore and get some literature that explains it completely. Better still, read the Gospel of John, and see for yourself what it is to be a Christian. Jesus told Nicodemus that "You must be born again." Those are Jesus' words (not Jimmy Carter's!) and they are still true today. Please, make certain of your credentials.

Again, this book has been addressed to Christian singles, for reasons explained in the preface. Parts of it certainly would be confusing and unbelievable to people who are not truly committed to Jesus Christ.

Now, in this chapter I want to touch on some issues we face as singles concerning our commitment to Christ. Once we do become Christians, we embark on a lifelong process of maturing into the reflection of Christ which should be our trademark as Christians. Though we never will fully arrive, we certainly can approach that goal if our hearts are fully committed to it.

Of course, every Christian everywhere faces obstacles to his or her Christian growth. These obstacles come from three sources: the world system and its unbiblical philosophies and thinking; our avowed enemy, Satan, and his demonic forces who currently rule this world system; and our own sinful flesh which is by nature self-centered and "prone to wander." The single Christian faces these same three enemies, just like everyone else.

I would simply like to point out some roadblocks to our spiritual growth which are somewhat unique to singles, because of our life-style and our circumstances. These are simply warning signs we should look for, to keep our feet on the right path.

Mistake: We fail to use our gifts fully in the Body of Christ.

We know from Scripture that all of us have been given gifts as defined and described in Romans 12 and 1 Corinthians 12 and 14, and 1 Peter 4:10 tells us that "Each one should use whatever gift he has received to serve others, faithfully administering God's grace in its various forms." In order for the Body of Christ (which is another Bible term for all true believers) to work as intended by God, these gifts must be exercised by each of us in the places where God has put us. When one part of the Body fails to use its gift, then the Body doesn't function as efficiently and effectively as it should.

For various reasons, Christian singles often do not use their gifts in church settings. One reason is that many churches don't consider singles "legitimate" members of the group. We are often viewed as fringe elements by others in the church, so we're not asked to do things for which we are totally equipped and qualified. I'll cover this problem more completely in the next chapter.

When we find ourselves in that kind of predicament, we have some decisions to make if we want to use our gifts in our local church setting. The worse thing we can decide to do is to neglect our gifts. We are accountable to God for the use of these gifts, and I don't think it will be acceptable to God for us to say, "Well, you see, Lord, the reason I didn't use that gift You gave me was that my church had a wrong attitude toward singles, and they didn't allow me to use it." Sounds a little weak, don't you think?

Sometimes you need someone who'll be first to start new traditions in these settings, where change is viewed with great skepticism and alarm. A proposal to the board, a conversation with the pastor, an offer to take a responsibility—many times a little effort is all it takes. I've been surprised at the results when I've stuck my neck out to question the status quo. It's actually caused some change to start happening.

Of course, you have to earn your right to be heard, and certainly the way you approach these trailblazing efforts is extremely critical. Remember Proverbs 16:21: "The wise in heart will be called discerning, and sweetness of speech increases persuasiveness" (NAS). But I would encourage you to be more assertive about finding ways to use your gifts in the local assembly where you serve, and to try to change some of those wrong perceptions about singles and their place in the Body.

Another reason we don't use our gifts as we should is that, again, we tend to see ourselves in a waiting room while we're single, and once we get married, we then become eligible to use our gifts. We've allowed this old mind-set to infiltrate our own thinking. I will say it very clearly: Singleness is not a handicap to serving the Lord.

In fact, incredible as it may seem, the Apostle Paul gives us clear indication in 1 Corinthians 7 that a single person has more opportunity to serve the Lord wholeheartedly than a married person. Only twice do I ever remember hearing anyone speak on this chapter, both times in radio messages. It's not exactly a comfortable chapter to consider, since it is at cross-purposes with a great deal of our thinking, for singles and marrieds alike. But to the credit of the speakers I heard, both of whom are married men, they told it like it was, without watering down the message of 1 Corinthians 7.

Quite simply, that chapter says that if you remain single, whatever state of singleness you are in, you can serve the Lord with greater freedom and less hindrance. In order for a marriage to work, two people have to be committed to working at the marriage, and that takes time. First Corinthians 7 says a married woman has to be concerned about the affairs of her home and her husband, and likewise a married man must be concerned about pleasing his wife. Those are necessary ingredients for a good marriage, and they take time—lots of time.

As a single person, I don't have those time-consuming responsibilities. So I can use that time in direct service to the Lord, with no guilt feelings for neglecting a relationship, no worrying about someone else's feelings, no time lost in adjusting to someone else's schedule. You really can't deny the logic of Paul's argument. However, very few people give it serious consideration.

Now, I also recognize the balance of Scripture, which teaches that marriage is good, God ordained marriage, it is normal. But why do the scales have to tip in that direction?

Can't we come to accept that both singleness and marriage are truly good, and not continue to show favoritism toward marriage, when indeed the Bible does not give us a prejudiced view toward one or the other? I certainly don't want singleness to be elevated to some place of honor, but simply to be accepted, in the minds of both married and single people, as a perfectly normal life-style.

Bible teaching is clear on the single life-style, as you look at 1 Corinthians 7. It gives us an opportunity for greater, unhindered service to the Lord.

Of course, we Christian singles don't always use our singleness as a gift. In fact, most singles don't like to hear this, I've discovered. To some it seems as if we're condemned to a prison rather than allowed special freedoms and opportunities.

That's because we find it so difficult to understand servanthood. I am learning that the more my life is consumed with a desire to please Jesus and hear His "Well done," the less servanthood frightens me or turns me off, the more I appreciate 1 Corinthians 7 instead of dreading to be confronted with it again. But I'll admit I have found myself reading it and resenting it at times. "Why do singles have a call to self-denial that married people don't have?" "It's not fair for a single to be expected to be more of a servant than a married person."

Of course, that is just twisted thinking on my part. We all have the same call to servanthood; it just takes different forms. The requirements on me as a single are just somewhat different from those on people who are married. I watch my married friends and family members and I see them struggling with relationship problems I never have to face. I see them having to learn servanthood by giving in to their partners, getting along with their partners, serving their partners. That's no easier than my brand of serving.

I also think of Jesus' words to Simon Peter, when Peter asked why John didn't have to suffer exactly what he had to suffer. Jesus answered Peter: "If I want him to remain alive until I return, what is that to you? You must follow me" (John 21:22). There's no question that we don't all have the same level of suffering or sacrifice in this life, but you can be sure of one thing: God is fair. It may not be settled until eternity, but someday the scales will be balanced. We can trust His justice. Our job is simply to follow.

It's interesting to see how we fight the principle of death to ourselves, and yet that is the only way we will find the life and contentment and peace we desire. As I've often tried to communicate to single people, what we really need is peace and contentment. If we would believe that God can give us that even without marriage, then no one has to feel sorry for us because we're single. As long as we're contented and peaceful, what difference does it make? Yet many still refuse to believe that they can find contentment except by doing it their way. What a great mistake we make when we try to tell God what is best for us.

Mistake: We fail to demonstrate hospitality as we should.

My dearest friends, Fran and her husband, Dick, have taught me much about the need for and the benefits of showing hospitality to people. They are very gifted in this way and have touched many lives simply by opening their home to so many people through the years.

But whether we are particularly gifted or not, whether we are married or not, we are exhorted in Scripture to be hospitable people. Here are two verses that make this clear:

Offer hospitality to one another without grumbling.

1 Peter 4:9

Share with God's people who are in need. Practice hospitality.

Romans 12:13

I find many singles never really give a serious thought to entertaining, to inviting someone over for a meal, or opening their home or apartment to a friend in need. Again, there seems to be this mind-set that these are duties reserved for married people. (Parenthetically, many married people never demonstrate hospitality, either.)

You're missing a special joy if you're not using the resources God has given you in your home or apartment and your things. Those "things" may not be fancy, but believe me, it makes absolutely no difference. If you serve on paper plates, nobody really cares. The thing that matters is that you went out of your way to show hospitality.

Can you imagine how much closer and more united the Body of Christ would be if we all practiced hospitality freely? Just by getting together more often, sharing our hearts, we would start to know and care about each other more. That would stop a lot of the backbiting and gossip that is too prevalent in Christian circles.

Did you ever notice how Jesus used social occasions to reach people? It's amazing what you can do over a meal. Just sitting around a table with food somehow creates an atmosphere that can be very warm and personal. It helps break down barriers to communication. It helps us reach out to others, in very simple ways.

This is not limited to women. You men can order pizza with great skill; I've seen you do it! Some of you can even cook spaghetti, grill hamburgers, or prepare gourmet meals! Remember, hospitality is not just for women. It applies to all of us.

Mistake: We allow relationships to control our commitment to Christ.

Many singles' spiritual lives run hot or cold, depending on the special people in their lives at the moment. When you spend a lot of time with people who are not truly committed to Jesus Christ, you rarely bring them up to your level; usually they bring you down to theirs. Especially in man/woman relationships.

I'm not talking, of course, about discipling someone, where you're helping him or her grow spiritually. A person who wants to be discipled is different from one who has no desire for spiritual things, never wants to talk about the Lord, seldom prays, looks for excuses to stay away from church, and generally shows little or no interest in things that relate to God.

Because of the desperateness singles often feel to find companionship and have a special person in their lives, many relinquish their commitment and lower their standards in order to keep the relationship going. Of course, that always leads to disastrous results.

I know what I'm talking about, because during my ten years of doing my own thing, I went with people who were not serious about God. But I wasn't going to allow that minor detail to prevent me from having a "meaningful relationship." Not once did I ever influence any of those people for the Lord. Quite the contrary, I did things and went places that were unquestionably compromising in order to be with them, to please them, to impress them.

It's not only romantic relationships which can influence us wrongly, but also peer relationships at work, or friends who do not share our faith in Christ. It is very easy to want to be part of the group, not look different, not be odd-person-out, so we let down our Christian standards in order to accommodate our relationships.

As disciples of Jesus Christ, we must let everything in our lives take second place to our commitment to Him. Otherwise we are not truly disciples. Discipleship is costly. Jesus made no bones about it. In fact, when people offered to be His disciples, He would always give them fair warning about the price tag. And many, upon hearing the cost, turned around and went away.

When you live your life without eternal eyes, you will always choose against discipleship, because the price will appear to be too high. But when you live with eternal values stamped on your eyelids, remembering that this life is *very* short and eternity is forever, discipleship will be the biggest bargain you can imagine. So what if I am not accepted by some others here on this earth? If I am storing up treasures in heaven, can anything else compare in importance?

In the final analysis, what everything comes down to is the Lordship of Jesus Christ in our lives. Are we soldiers of the Cross or not? When that issue is settled, and Jesus is Lord, relationships will not interfere with our commitment to Christ. Indeed, our commitment may interfere dramatically with certain relationships. It is sometimes one of the costs of discipleship.

11

Common Mistakes Others Make in Their Attitudes Toward Singles

An attractive single woman in one of my focus groups told me a story that illustrates a very common problem singles face with nonsingle people in their lives. She formerly attended a church in her hometown where she had grown up before coming to our church in the city. She loved her congregation; it was home to her. But for whatever reason the church had no Sunday school class for singles or career people. So in order to attend Sunday school, which she had done all her life, her only option was a class of married women taught by her pastor's wife.

One Sunday she didn't feel really well, so she decided to attend only the Sunday morning service and skip Sunday school. When she arrived at church for the service, the pastor's wife came up to her and said, "Oh, I'm so sorry you weren't in Sunday school today; we really missed you." My friend first thought she was simply missed, but her teacher went on to say, "I was hoping you'd be there today because I knew you could really contribute to the lesson. We talked about loneliness."

The underlying assumption: All singles are lonely;

married people are not. As this lovely woman told the story to us, I could hear and feel the pain; all of us empathized with her, because we've been there. We have endured those comments and attitudes that say to us in one way or another, "You're not exactly right; something's wrong; you're still single."

When I hear these stories—and I hear plenty of them— I lose my cool easily. I want to scream, "Don't do that to us! PLEASE, don't injure us with your words and attitudes. Just treat us like regular, normal people. That's all we ask!"

So, I've been looking forward to writing this chapter, because I intend to "ventilate" my feelings on this subject. What worries me is that since this book is directed to singles, only singles will read this chapter. I hope you who are single will find ways to get the appropriate people to read this, because they need to hear it.

Mistakes of married people toward singles.

More and more I'm convinced that the gulf between married and single people, especially in our Christian circles, is harmful. Why have we allowed it to happen? The Apostle Paul clearly tells us that in the Body of Christ there is no division of any kind (Galatians 3:28). Yet, so often you can almost feel the dividing line invisibly drawn between those who are single and those who are married in our Christian society.

There's blame enough to go around for this lack of understanding. Earlier in this book I've encouraged the singles to actively work at eliminating the division. Now, I hope some married people will read this and be willing to help in the process as well.

The first mistake married people make toward us singles is in their attitude. Many of you view our single status as a second-class citizenship, and your comments tell us that we're not quite okay yet because we're not married.

One single person related to me recently that married friends will frequently say to her, "I just want you to know I'm praying that God will send you a mate." She said, "I wonder, would they pray for me if I were not single? Is that the only need they see in my life?"

Please, don't say that to us! Pray for us, yes, but pray that God will be our highest priority, that our lives will be totally yielded to Jesus Christ, that we'll know His guidance in all our decisions, that we'll find our completeness in Him. But don't voluntarily offer your prayers simply that we will be married. The message that gets through to us when you do that is: "When you are finally married, you'll be okay."

If a single person specifically asks you to pray that he or she will find a godly mate, then please do. There's nothing wrong with that prayer, as long as it is not a consuming desire. For years I prayed for my daughter before she ever met her husband, Todd, that if in God's plan she was to be married, God would begin early on to prepare both of them for each other. As I've told Todd, I prayed for him specifically before I knew his name. But my prayer was not one of fear that my daughter might not be married. It was a prayer for guidance and preparation, if indeed marriage was to be a reality for her.

After all, it actually might be God's highest purpose for us to remain single. No one but God can determine which life-style is His choice. It is a biblical choice to make and for some people, singleness is God's highest calling. Don't assume that marriage is the best thing for every single person. It may not be true. Read 1 Corinthians 7 again, until you really start to believe that the single life can be a high calling, not a curse.

Another attitude we frequently see and hear is that of pity for singles. A good example is the story I related at the beginning of this chapter. Married people assume we singles are lonely. Not necessarily so. Aloneness does not automatically mean lonely. Many singles' lives are full and running over with meaningful activities and relationships. Quite honestly, many of us really enjoy our own company!

I think of Karen Shafland, a dear, lovely single woman who is a speech therapist for a local school board. She is continually giving herself to others, sharing her life with others, doing things for others. Karen is being used by God to touch many people in many ways. I seriously doubt that she has much time to be lonely. I can think of many married people who live much lonelier lives than Karen.

Would she like to find a life-mate someday? My guess is she would. She's as normal as blueberry pie. But I've never heard her complain about it. It isn't the first topic of conversation when you get near her. She is not consumed with her singleness; she's too busy sending eternal treasures ahead of her to heaven by investing her time in other people. There are many, many single Christians like Karen. We're not that rare a breed.

So, please don't feel sorry for us. That just adds to the division between us. You might even let us know you "envy" our life-styles in some way (which I'm sure you do). There's nothing wrong in each of us appreciating the good things about the other life-style, without being discontent. Certainly we singles appreciate the good things that marriage offers—companionship, parenthood, sexual relationships. But I know that married people must also secretly, if not openly, appreciate some of our freedom, our flexibility as single people.

Each life-style has its assets and liabilities, but it seems to me that we accept the liabilities of the married life-style more easily than we do the single life-style. Won't you please help us appreciate what we have as single people rather than magnifying the negatives? I hope we can do the same for you. I think that's part of what it means to be an encourager.

Another mistake married people can make is trying to play matchmaker for us. I think this happens especially to men. Somehow married people (particularly women) just can't bear to see a single man unattached!

Now, I'm not talking about simple introductions, when it is the natural thing to do. I'm referring to the all-out efforts married people sometimes make to get two people together.

Matchmaking can be disastrous in many ways. First, you can be meddling in God's business. You really have to think twice before you start to maneuver people because it looks like a "good match" to you. If you think there are possibilities in a relationship, just pray about it a great deal. God is very capable of doing the maneuvering, and when He does it, it is always at the right time and in the right way.

Second, matchmaking continues to send us that negative message: "As soon as you get married, you'll be okay. Something's wrong with being single."

Third, you can cause some very uncomfortable experiences for those single people and raise unrealistic expectations.

I heard a story about a single woman who was dearly loved by her married friends, who were very anxious for her to find a man, assuming that would be the greatest thing that could happen to her. One day one of those married couples met what seemed to them to be the perfect man for her. He was the right age, right credentials—and he was single! So, with good but very misguided intentions, they urgently called her and told her to be in a certain place at a certain time so they could introduce her. They were arranging a "casual" introduction.

She was excited that finally there was a single eligible man who offered potential. Her expectations were raised; her hopes were built. She showed up at the appointed time; he didn't.

The story goes on, but suffice it to say she went through some emotional trauma—totally unnecessarily—because some well-intentioned friends started meddling and set her up for embarrassment and disappointment. I could feel the hair on my neck start to rise when I heard the story. Please don't do those things to us!

We appreciate your concern; we need your love, but not your pity. Don't keep sending us the message that we're not okay until we're married.

How often do we hear comments like: "How could a good-looking man like you not be married?" or, "You're so pretty; what's the matter with those men in your church?" Please, don't say such things to us, and don't say those things behind our backs. Please try to change your own attitude toward us. If you keep thinking that singleness is not God's best for us, your attitude will keep showing through. First you have to change the way you think about us, and that will change the things you say to us and the way you treat us.

Mistakes of family members toward singles.

Certainly the things I've described in the preceding section can apply to family members very appropriately. In addition, though, there are some mistakes peculiar to family members, and I'd like to address those.

I've noticed that sometimes family members can expect the singles in the family unit to carry more family responsibility because they are single. For example, if there is a sick parent, the married siblings sometimes expect the single brothers or sisters to put life on hold, move to another location, or take the incapacitated parent into their home since they don't have families themselves to worry about. I think you need to be careful to spread the responsibility around evenly. At least make a very sincere offer, and if the single person really wants to make those sacrifices, then you can find other ways to try to distribute the responsibility.

Remember, we single people need family support just as much as anyone else, maybe more. My family is so wonderful about including me in the group and never showing any differentiation, even though I'm the only single sibling. There were some adjustments when I first was divorced, but a little time and a lot of love have overcome those uncomfortable feelings. I never feel like an odd man out at family affairs, nor do I feel any pity for me on their part (perhaps, in part because I don't feel sorry for myself). At any rate, that family support is one of the most important elements in my life. It gives me a feeling of wholeness and completeness, without which I just don't know where I'd be.

Of course, that's true for all of us, isn't it? Sometimes families give us that support, sometimes they don't, whether we're married or single. I am particularly blessed by God to have the family I have. My heart goes out to those who do not. The letters I receive tell me that the lack of family support and inclusion is one of the toughest emotional deprivations to handle. I always thank God that as Christians, even when our family is not what it should be, the love of Jesus Christ can fill in all those missing pieces.

Mistakes of church members, leaders, and staff toward singles.

Think of the governing body in your church, whatever you call it: Executive Committee, Trustees, Deacons,

Board of Directors. How many single people are members of that board? If there is one, it is unusual. If singles are fairly represented according to the number of singles in the congregation, it is extremely unusual. In most churches, singles are grossly underrepresented in church affairs. The single adult population is a large percentage of most congregations, sometimes even the majority, and yet all too often they are not even considered for positions of leadership in the church simply because they're not married.

That is beginning to change, thank God. I can see it happening, little by little. But change is slow, isn't it? I guess, for us singles, it is another opportunity to learn patience!

While it is not my intention to get into theological discussions here, I cannot imagine how you would scripturally justify discrimination against singles for positions of leadership in the church simply because they are not married. I'm certain that in many churches there is no intention of discrimination, it just happens. When the nominating committees meet, the names of singles just don't come up.

Can I say it again? Please read 1 Corinthians 7 and believe that singleness can be a choice—God's choice—for enhanced, not diminished, service to God. If you are disallowing singles to serve in legitimate roles where they have gifts and are qualified, you are missing important pieces in your local body, important contributions by these single people. And you are forcing them to find parachurch groups that will accept and appreciate their gifts.

I've heard comments by members in the church, usually older members, truly disparaging singles simply because they are not married. I suppose only time will cure some of these things, but it hurts so much to hear one part of the Body of Christ discount the validity and rights of another part of the Body of Christ.

I think one of the most marvelous things about being a Christian is the oneness we have with each other, regardless of our labels, our circumstances, our backgrounds. How often I've been a part of a group of very diverse Christians, and the differences simply faded as we shared our unity in Jesus Christ. How enriching those experiences are! How we need more of them!

Can't we just forget the married and single name tags that seem to be written on our foreheads at times, and just get to know and love each other because we're all a part of the family of God? Of course we can. That's how the Body of Christ is intended to operate. When it fails to do so, we all miss out on great blessings.